UNIVERSITY CHALLENGE

—— THE ——

ULTIMATE QUESTIONS

Compiled by
Steve Tribe

quadrille

First published in 2016 by Quadrille

Foreword by Peter Gwyn
Text © *University Challenge*™ and ITV Ventures Limited 2016.
University Challenge™ is produced in association with
The College Bowl Company.

Quadrille is an imprint of Hardie Grant www.hardiegrant.com.au

Quadrille Publishing
Pentagon House
52–54 Southwark Street
London SE1 1UN
www.quadrille.co.uk

ISBN 978 184949 895 1

British Library Cataloguing-in-Publication Data. A catalogue record
for this book is available from the British Library.

Publishing Director: Sarah Lavelle
Art Director: Helen Lewis
Designer and Editor: Steve Tribe
Cover Designer: Emily Lapworth

Printed and bound in China

10 9 8 7 6 5 4 3 2 1

Contents

Foreword

Looking back at the earliest editions of *University Challenge*, broadcast in 1962 in rather grainy black and white, it's tempting to wonder what the students of that era would have thought if they'd known that their children and grandchildren would be able to find the answer to almost any question, however difficult, by accessing Google Search on their mobile phones.

If the programme and its viewers agree on one thing, it's . perhaps that there really *is* such a thing as General Knowledge: a range of facts, dates, names, areas of awareness, cultural references and much, much more, all of which helps us to make sense of the world. There's a shared belief that General Knowledge is a good thing to have, that having more of it is better than having less, that it's fun to test how much we've got, and that young people who possess it in glorious abundance deserve to be celebrated. Furthermore, the best of them should be given a trophy, along with the right to call themselves *University Challenge* Series Champions. Underpinning all of this is the old-fashioned belief that true General Knowledge belongs in the brain, not in the list of results from an internet search.

It's not only an extraordinary range and depth of knowledge that our most accomplished students demonstrate, but also an ability to spot the direction in which a question is going, and the precise moment when they have heard sufficient information to be sure they have the correct answer. At times, this ability is quite eerie, as on the distant occasion when, having heard Bamber Gascoigne utter only the words

'On what colourful occasion', a contestant buzzed in with the correct answer of 'The Field of the Cloth of Gold', no doubt prompting millions of viewers to brush up on their sixteenth-century history.

Speechlessness is not a term one would readily associate with Jeremy Paxman, but he was once rendered close to it after asking the question: 'What day of the week will it be one hundred days after Monday?' The programme's production team expected baffled faces all round, but one contestant promptly buzzed in with the correct answer: 'Wednesday'. 'How on earth did you know that?' asked Jeremy, after a stunned pause. 'It's easy,' replied the contestant, 'if you know modular arithmetic.' 'For weeks afterwards,' Jeremy told me later, 'I had people stopping me in the street asking me how on earth he knew that.' This perhaps just demonstrates that an easy question is one to which you happen to know the answer.

In the pages that follow, you'll encounter thousands of questions taken from past editions of *University Challenge*, some rather hard, some perhaps a little less so, but never, we hope, too obscure; we do quite genuinely try and avoid those questions that very occasionally prompt Jeremy Paxman to say 'but *why* you should be expected to know that, I have no idea,' before tossing the offending question-card over his shoulder.

We hope you enjoy them.

Peter Gwyn
Executive Producer, *University Challenge*

'If anyone says it's a jolly day
out, I'd think they were lying.
On a scale of one to ten of how
competitive we were? About ten.'

IAN HISLOP
(Editor, *Private Eye*)
Contestant, 2005

'I was 27 when we did the
auditions for the presenter's role.
And of course the students were
only 21 or whatever, and at that
age, at six years' difference, I was
the Old Man of the Hills – I knew
everything, and they were just
undergraduates!'

BAMBER GASCOIGNE
Presenter, 1962–1987

Match One

1 What letter and number denote the vitamin which is also the designated food colour E101? It imparts a yellow-orange colour to commercial vitamin supplements.

Three bonus questions on Quakers

a. Raised as a Quaker on the farm of his aunt, which Hollywood actor became the first to be nominated posthumously for an Academy Award as Best Actor after his death in 1955?

b. A statue to Joseph Pease, the railway pioneer who became the first Quaker MP, stands in which town of north-east England, where he was born in 1799?

c. Born into a Quaker family in Cumberland, which scientist published his atomic theory in the 1808 work *A New System of Chemical Philosophy*?

2 Founded in 1961, the I.U.G.S. is a body devoted to international cooperation in which field of science?

Three bonus questions on quantum physics

a. Heisenberg's original uncertainty relation concerned which two observable properties of a particle?

b. Quantitatively, the product of the two uncertainties is always greater than or equal to the unreduced Planck constant, h, divided by what number?

c. A similar uncertainty relationship exists between energy and what quantity?

3 What two-digit number links the first part of the small intestine, the number of cranial nerves, and the atomic number of magnesium?

> **Three bonus questions on pairs of names. In each case, the surname of the first person described is the given name of the second, for example 'Jane Austen' and 'Austen Chamberlain'. Your answer must include the given name and surname of both people described.**
>
> **a.** The eighteenth-century inventor of the marine chronometer now known as H4, and the actor whose film roles include John Book in *Witness* and Rick Deckard in *Blade Runner*?
>
> **b.** The author of *The World According to Garp*, and the composer of 'White Christmas'?
>
> **c.** The broadcaster and author whose works include *Cultural Amnesia*, and the navigator who landed at Botany Bay in 1770?

4 Founded in 1971 by Michael Stern Hart, which internet project provides free online access to thousands of e-books, and is named after a German pioneer of printing who died in 1468?

> **Three bonus questions on films of the 1940s. In each case, name the film in which the following lines are spoken.**
>
> **a.** 'Faith is believing when common sense tells you not to. Don't you see? It's not just Kris that's on trial, it's everything he stands for. It's kindness and joy and love and all the other intangibles.'

b. 'We always were English, and we always will be English; and it's just because we are English that we're sticking up for our right to be Burgundians!'

c. 'I don't think any word can explain a man's life. No, I guess Rosebud is just a piece in a jigsaw puzzle. A missing piece.'

5 The figure of which ancient Greek god appears in the wedding procession of Theseus and Hippolyta in *The Two Noble Kinsmen*, attributed to Shakespeare and Fletcher? In *As You Like It*, he restores Rosalind to her father and performs the nuptial ritual.

Three bonus questions on Chinese history

a. Born around 45 BCE, the short rule of the usurper Wang divides the 'Western' and 'Eastern' periods of which Chinese dynasty?

b. An Lushan was a general of Central Asian descent who rebelled against which dynasty? Though suppressed, the rebellion caused great loss of life and a weakening of central authority.

c. The Taiping and Nian rebellions were major disturbances during which Chinese dynasty?

6 Also known as the Cryptozoic, what term, deriving in part from a Latin name for Wales, denotes the span of geological time that preceded the Phanerozoic eon?

Three bonus questions on geological periods

a. Which period of the Palaeozoic era is named after an ancient people of north Wales?

b. Which period of the Palaeozoic era is named after a region of Russia to the west of the Ural mountains?

c. Which period of the Palaeozoic era is named after a county of southern England?

7 What annual event was held at the Baltic Gallery in Gateshead in 2011 and in Derry in Northern Ireland in 2013, these being the first times since its inception in 1984 that it has taken place outside a Tate gallery?

Three bonus questions on landlocked countries

a. Which South American country lost its coastline as a result of the War of the Pacific of 1879–1883?

b. The breakup of the former Yugoslavia left three countries that do not have a coastline. One is Kosovo. What are the other two?

c. Which African country lost its coastline when Eritrea gained its independence in 1993?

8 'That, like a wounded snake, drags its slow length along.' Also known as iambic hexameter, in which metre is this line from Pope's *Essay on Criticism* written? It takes its name from that of a ruler of antiquity.

Three bonus questions on world rulers. I will read a list of rulers who were on the throne or in power during the first year of a given century. In each case, I simply want the century.

a. Vasudeva I of the Kushan Empire, Vologases V of Parthia, and the Roman emperor Septimius Severus?

b. Yohl Ik'nal, queen of the Maya city of Palenque, the Byzantine emperor Maurice, and Empress Suiko of Japan?

c. Charles the Simple of France, Arpad, Grand Prince of the Hungarians, and Edward the Elder, King of the Anglo-Saxons?

9 After the then reigning monarch, what three-word name was given to a fund aimed at supplementing the income of less wealthy Anglican clergy? It was established in 1704.

Three bonus questions on the 1923 general election

a. Which future prime minister entered parliament for the first time in 1923 as the member for Warwick and Leamington?

b. Later prime minister, who was re-elected as MP for Limehouse in 1923? He held the seat until 1950.

c. That election saw which future prime minister stand for the last time as a Liberal at Leicester West, where he was defeated by the Labour candidate?

10 What name links the title of a 2001 novel by W.G. Sebald, a Parisian railway station, a battle of 1805 also known as the Battle of the Three Emperors, and the original surname of the dancer Fred Astaire?

Three bonus questions on cycling

a. 'The man who is learning how to ride a bicycle has no advantage over the non-cyclist in the struggle for existence.' Which playwright made this assertion in *Back to Methuselah*?

b. In the 1927 work *An Outline of Philosophy*, which English philosopher compared the acquisition of speech to learning to ride a bicycle?

c. Commenting on a bicycle crash that happened when Shaw collided with Russell in 1895, the latter later suggested that he thought Shaw regarded the 'incident as proof of the virtues of' which dietary practice?

11 Give the specific name of the component of an electric circuit that converts alternating current into direct current by allowing current to flow through it in one direction only.

Three bonus questions on an economist

a. The Canadian-born US economist Myron S. Scholes shared the 1997 Nobel Prize with Robert C. Merton for a new method of determining the value of which financial contracts, their name being a generic term for futures, options and swaps?

b. Along with Scholes, who gives his name to an options pricing model that led to the development of a major new financial market? It enables traders to diversify risk.

c. Scholes has been called the 'intellectual father' of which instrument, an insurance-like contract that promises to cover losses on certain securities in the event of a default?

12 In which US state is Springer Mountain, the southern terminus of the Appalachian trail?

Three bonus questions on classical music

a. Meaning 'sung' in Italian, what term describes a musical composition, often using a sacred text, comprising recitatives, arias and choruses?

b. Which scenic cantata was based on texts from the Middle Ages that were rediscovered in a Bavarian monastery in 1803? It opens with the movement 'Fortuna Imperatrix Mundi'.

c. Which English composer wrote the 1907 cantata *Toward the Unknown Region*, with words by Walt Whitman? His other cantatas include *Willow-Wood*.

13 What adjective may describe both a star with an unusually high velocity, and an electron that acquires energy from an electric field at a greater rate than it loses through particle collision?

Three bonus questions on astronomy

a. The Helix Nebula, the Saturn Nebula and the yellow supergiant Sadalmelik are all found in which constellation of the Zodiac?

b. Serpentarius, meaning 'snake-holder', is a former name of which constellation that straddles the celestial equator? It is the location of Barnard's Star.

c. Sagittarius A* is an astronomical radio source in the centre of our galaxy and is believed to be the location of what kind of object, which in this case has a mass of between two and five million times that of the Sun?

14 'From a private gentlewoman he made me a marchioness, from a marchioness a queen, and now he hath left no higher degree of honour, he gives my innocency the crown of martyrdom.' These are the words of which royal figure, shortly before her death in 1536?

Three bonus questions on queens and their lovers

a. David Riccio was an Italian courtier murdered at Holyroodhouse in Edinburgh in 1566 when he was suspected of being the lover of which queen?

b. Francis Dereham and Thomas Culpeper were accused of being the lovers of which English queen, who was executed in 1542?

c. Which English king, who ruled from 1302, is traditionally believed to have been brutally murdered by his wife Isabella and her lover Roger Mortimer in 1327?

15 Subtitled 'The London Charivari', which illustrated weekly periodical was founded in 1841, had its publication suspended in 1992, was revived in 1996, and finally closed in 2002?

Three bonus questions on graphic novels

a. 'It feels like a character I created thirty years ago has escaped the realm of fiction.' Which writer said this, referring to the sight of global protesters adopting the Guy Fawkes mask worn by the protagonist of his *V for Vendetta*?

b. Although the illustrator Eddie Campbell believes otherwise, in the comic series *From Hell* Alan Moore identifies the royal physician Sir William Withey Gull as which notorious figure?

c. First published in 1999, which comic book series by Alan Moore features an eponymous team of secret agents that includes Edward Hyde, Captain Nemo, the Invisible Man and Allan Quatermain?

16 In which Italian city are the Palazzo Madama and the Castello del Valentino? Along with other buildings, they form part of a UNESCO World Heritage Site known as 'Residences of the Royal House of Savoy'.

Three bonus questions on kings of Scotland. In each case, give the century that saw the reigns of the following.

a. Duncan I, Macbeth and Malcolm Canmore?

b. Alexander II, Alexander III and John de Balliol?

c. James I, II and III?

17 Listen carefully and give a three-word answer. The chemical symbols for uranium and antimony may be concatenated to give the abbreviation for which piece of computer technology?

Three bonus questions on fictional planets. In each case, name the author who created the following.

a. Caladan, Chusuk, Parmentier and Arrakis?

b. Urras, Davenant, Rokanan and Gethen?

c. Kalgan, Helicon, Askone, Trantor and Terminus?

18 An internet meme named after a reference work first published in 1852, the first rule of what fictitious 'club' is that you do not confer, chat, converse, verbalise, vocalise, mention, babble, spill the beans, squeal, let the cat out of the bag or allude to it?

Three bonus questions on museums

a. In 2010 it was announced that the National Football Museum would move to Manchester from Deepdale, which claims to be the world's oldest professional football venue. In which city is Deepdale?

b. A museum in Huntingdon is named after and dedicated to which historical figure, born in the town in 1599?

c. In which English city is the International Slavery Museum, opened in 2007 to mark the bicentenary of the abolition of the British slave trade?

19 Which historian presented the BBC's annual Reith Lectures in 2012? Born in Scotland, his works include *The Ascent of Money* and *Civilization: The West and the Rest.*

Three bonus questions on a stock exchange

a. NASDAQ became the world's first electronic stock exchange when it began trading in 1971. In which city is it located?

b. The first four letters of the acronym NASDAQ represent 'National Association of Securities Dealers'; for what do the last two letters stand?

c. In November 2007, NASDAQ bought which stock exchange, the oldest in America which had been in operation since 1790?

20 Obtained chiefly from trees of the genus *Boswellia*, native to the Middle East, olibanum is an alternative name for which aromatic gum resin?

Three bonus questions on a literary figure

a. 'All intellectual improvement arises from leisure.' These are the words of which literary figure, recorded in April 1773?

b. According to other words attributed by Boswell to Johnson, what act is 'not of importance, it lasts so short a time'?

c. Boswell reports that when Johnson was asked if a man could be happy in the present moment, he replied, 'Never, but when he is –' what?

21 On 6 August 2012, Gale Crater on Mars was the landing site for which NASA rover?

Three bonus questions on European history

a. Which major European city was besieged by Ottoman forces in 1529 and 1683, both times unsuccessfully?

b. Which sultan commanded the Ottoman army at the 1529 siege of Vienna?

    c.   Which Polish ruler commanded the combined force that lifted the siege of Vienna in 1683?

22 In mathematics, what is the lowest common multiple of all the prime numbers between 1 and 6?

Three bonus questions on shorter words that can be made using any of the eight letters of the word 'doggerel'. In each case, give the word from the definition.

    a.   The Latin word that comes between *cogito* and *sum* in the dictum proposed by René Descartes in 1637?

    b.   An S-shaped curve particularly associated with arches; it is a leitmotif of Alan Hollinghurst's novel *The Line of Beauty*.

    c.   The chief magistrate of Venice or Genoa until the late eighteenth century?

23 The decay of uranium-238 to thorium-234 is an instance of which form of ionising radiation?

Three bonus questions on the collection of the British Library

    a.   Made in 868, and described by the British Library as 'the earliest complete survival of a dated printed book', the 'Diamond Sutra' was discovered in a sealed cave in which country?

    b.   Surviving in a single medieval manuscript in the collection of the British Library, what is the oldest epic poem in Old English?

    c.   Produced in the middle of the fourth century, the 'Codex Sinaiticus' is one of the two earliest Christian Bibles, and is handwritten in which language?

24 On 25 December 1991, who resigned as president of the Union of Soviet Socialist Republics, at the same time that this polity was dissolved?

Three bonus questions on human anatomy

a. The plantar fascia is a fibrous band that helps to maintain the structure and shape of which part of the human body?

b. What collective name is given to the seven rounded bones in the foot, including the cuboid, talus, and calcaneus?

c. From a Greek term also applied to a body of close-order infantry, what name denotes the fourteen bones found in the toes?

25 'Friends forever' in 1992, 'Share the spirit' in 2000, 'Welcome home' in 2004, 'One world, one dream' in 2008 and 'Inspire a generation' in 2012 have all been mottos for what event?

Three bonus questions on explorers

a. Born in 1394, Prince Henry, the son of John I of Portugal, is usually known by what nickname because of the number of sea expeditions he financed?

b. Until it was renamed Maputo in 1976, the capital of Mozambique was named after which Portuguese explorer, who visited the city in the sixteenth century?

c. Which Portuguese explorer was killed in the region of the Philippines after landing there in his flagship the Trinidad in 1521?

26 What bird links: a dance set to ragtime music, popular in the early twentieth century; a serious and forthright discussion; a method of curing addiction by abrupt cessation; and a brand of processed meat that shot to notoriety after Jamie Oliver campaigned to have it removed from school menus?

Three bonus questions on optical illusions

a. What type of building gives its name to an optical illusion in which a rotating object appears to spin in the opposite direction when viewed at an angle in silhouette from long distance?

b. What surname is that of an English father and son, the latter a noted mathematician, and is given to diagrams popularised by them in which a triangle and a staircase represent physically impossible objects?

c. An optical phenomenon in which a photograph is viewed upside down, but with the eyes and mouth in the original orientation, takes its name from which prime minister?

27 The founder of one of the tribes of Israel, who, according to the Book of Genesis, was the first-born son of Leah and Jacob?

Three bonus questions on biological chemistry

a. Which metal is found in chlorophyll molecules?

b. The oxygen-carrying component in the blood of an octopus contains what transition metal?

c. What is the name of the only naturally occurring amino acid in which the amino acid component forms part of a ring?

28 'I am the wife of Mao Tse-Tung' is an aria from which opera? With a libretto by Alice Goodman and music by John Adams, it is based on a US president's historic diplomatic visit in 1972.

Three bonus questions on names, all of which begin with the same three letters

a. A fourteenth-century Italian populist who incited the citizens of Rome to rebel against the nobles? He is the title character of Wagner's first significant opera.

b. Born in 1826, which German mathematician gives his name both to a branch of geometry also known as 'elliptic' and to a major unsolved hypothesis concerning the Zeta Function?

c. A German film-maker, best known for *Triumph of the Will*, a depiction of the Nazi rallies in Nuremberg in 1934?

29 Which president of South Africa shared the Nobel Peace Prize with Nelson Mandela in 1993?

Three bonus questions on a Japanese author

a. *What I Talk About When I Talk About Running* is a 2008 memoir by which Japanese novelist?

b. Which of Murakami's novels had two English translators working on it in order to speed up publication, and also saw bookshops in the UK and the US opening at midnight for its release in 2011?

c. Published in Japanese in 1987, Murakami's fifth novel is named after which song by The Beatles?

30 Listen carefully. The names of three counties of England and Wales appear in the names of UK national parks. For ten points, name two of them.

Three bonus questions on oaths

a. From the improvised meeting-place in which it took place, what name is commonly given to the oath sworn in June 1789 by which the representatives of the French third estate refused to disperse until Louis XVI accepted a new constitution?

b. Sentenced in 1834 to transportation for seven years for administering illegal oaths, George Loveless and five other Dorset farmworkers are known collectively by what name?

c. Regarded as a defining work of the neo-classical style in art, *The Oath of the Horatii* is among the works of which French painter, born in 1748?

> 'Bamber Gascoigne seemed
> the perfect professorial figure:
> urbane, and incredibly well read –
> but wise and gentle as well. A sort
> of Obi Wan Kenobi figure.'
>
> DAVID NICHOLLS
> Author, *Starter for Ten*

The Answers

1 B2 (riboflavin)
    a.   James Dean (He was nominated in both 1955 and 1956 for his performances in East of Eden and Giant.)
    b.   Darlington
    c.   (John) Dalton

2 Geology / Earth Science (The International Union of Geological Sciences)
    a.   Position and momentum
    b.   Four pi
    c.   Time

3 Twelve
    a.   John Harrison and Harrison Ford
    b.   John Irving and Irving Berlin
    c.   Clive James and James Cook

4 (Project) Gutenberg
    a.   *Miracle on 34th Street* (1947; not 'Miracle on 42nd Street', which is a track by The Flaming Lips)
    b.   *Passport to Pimlico* (1949)
    c.   *Citizen Kane* (1941)

5 Hymen
    a.   Han (206 BCE–220 CE)
    b.   Tang (618–907 CE; An Lushan rebellion 755–763 CE)
    c.   Ch'ing / Qing (1644–1912, 1917; accept 'Manchu', qualifying it)

6 Precambrian (from the Latin Cambria; not Cambrian)
- **a.** Ordovician (the Ordovices; not 'Silurian', the Silures lived in South Wales)
- **b.** Permian
- **c.** Devonian

7 (The) Turner Prize (Exhibition)
- **a.** Bolivia (annexed by Chile)
- **b.** Serbia and Macedonia (Bosnia's coastline is only 20km long; Croatia's is almost 1,700km, excluding islands; Slovenia's coastline is 43km long)
- **c.** Ethiopia

8 Alexandrine (poetic metre of twelve syllables; 'A needless Alexandrine ends the song' is the preceding line)
- **a.** Third century
- **b.** Seventh century
- **c.** Tenth century

9 Queen Anne's Bounty
- **a.** (Anthony) Eden (Macmillan stood unsuccessfully at Stockton-on-Tees and was elected there the following year; Chamberlain was MP for Birmingham Ladywood, 1918–1929)
- **b.** (Clement) Attlee
- **c.** (Winston) Churchill

10 Austerlitz
- **a.** (George Bernard) Shaw
- **b.** (Bertrand) Russell
- **c.** Vegetarianism

11 Rectifier
- **a.** Derivatives
- **b.** (Fischer) Black (the Black-Scholes formula)
- **c.** Credit-default swap

12 Georgia
- **a.** Cantata
- **b.** *Carmina Burana* (by Carl Orff, of course)
- **c.** (Ralph) Vaughan Williams

13 Runaway
- **a.** Aquarius
- **b.** Ophiuchus
- **c.** Black hole

14 Anne Boleyn
- **a.** Mary, Queen of Scots
- **b.** Catherine Howard (Anne Boleyn was executed in 1536, of course)
- **c.** Edward II / Edward of Caernarvon

15 Punch
- **a.** Alan Moore
- **b.** Jack the Ripper
- **c.** *The League of Extraordinary Gentlemen*

16 Turin / Torino
- **a.** Eleventh (1034–1040; 1040–1057; 1058–1093)
- **b.** Thirteenth (1214–1249; 1249–1286; 1292–1296)
- **c.** Fifteenth (1406–1437; 1437–1460; 1460–1488)

17 Universal serial bus (U plus Sb, of course)
- **a.** Frank Herbert (in the *Dune* novels)
- **b.** Ursula K. Le Guin (in her *Hainish* novel sequence)
- **c.** Isaac Asimov (in the *Foundation* series)

18 Thesaurus (Club)
- **a.** Preston
- **b.** Oliver Cromwell
- **c.** Liverpool

19 Niall Ferguson
    a.   New York (City)
    b.   Automated Quotation(s) (accept 'Automatic Quotation(s) System)
    c.   Philadelphia (accept 'PHLX')

20 Frankincense (not myrrh, which is a different genus, i.e. *Commiphora*)
    a.   (Dr Samuel) Johnson
    b.   '(The act of) Dying'
    c.   'Drunk'

21 Curiosity
    a.   Vienna
    b.   Suleiman I / Suleiman the Magnificent
    c.   John (Jan) Sobieski / John III

22 30
    a.   *Ergo*
    b.   Ogee
    c.   Doge

23 Alpha (i.e. alpha radiation or alpha decay)
    a.   China (in the Mogao Caves near Dunhuang)
    b.   *Beowulf*
    c.   Greek

24 (Mikhail) Gorbachev
    a.   Foot (specifically, it supports the arch on the sole of the foot.)
    b.   Tarsals / tarsal bones / tarsus (not metatarsals, of course)
    c.   Phalanges

25 (Summer) Olympics
    a.   (Henry) the Navigator

    b.   Lourenço Marques
    c.   (Ferdinand) Magellan

26 Turkey (trot, talk, cold and Twizzler)
    a.   Windmill (the windmill illusion)
    b.   Penrose (after Lionel and Roger Penrose)
    c.   (Margaret) Thatcher

27 Reuben (Genesis 29: 31–32)
    a.   Magnesium
    b.   Copper
    c.   Proline

28 Nixon in China
    a.   (Cola di) Rienzi / Rienzo
    b.   (Bernhard) Riemann
    c.   (Leni) Riefenstahl

29 (F.W.) de Klerk
    a.   (Haruki) Murakami
    b.   *1Q84*
    c.   'Norwegian Wood'

30 Northumberland / Pembrokeshire (Coast) / Yorkshire (Dales) (Accept York, as in North York Moors, as it is a contraction of Yorkshire. Not Norfolk: the name of the national park is 'Broads' and it includes areas of Suffolk.)
    a.   The Tennis Court (Oath)
    b.   The Tolpuddle Martyrs
    c.   (Jacques-Louis) David

Match Two

1. Born in 1832, which French painter's name appeared in the official title of the first Post-Impressionist exhibition, organised by Roger Fry in 1910?

   ### Three bonus questions on human anatomy

   a. In which bone is the glenoid cavity found?

   b. The head of which bone articulates with the glenoid cavity?

   c. Which bone links the scapula with the sternum?

2. In compound nouns, what seven-letter gerund may follow words including 'frequency', 'bed', 'channel', 'bar', and 'island'? Alone, the same word may refer to the use of a traditional flavouring agent in beer.

   ### Three bonus questions on a shared prefix

   a. The condition known as nyctophobia indicates an extreme or irrational fear of what?

   b. Nyctalopia, or night-blindness, can be caused by a deficiency of which vitamin?

   c. To what does the term nyctanthous refer?

3. Which play by Shakespeare includes these lines: 'Love looks not with the eyes, but with the mind, / And therefore is winged cupid painted blind'?

Three bonus questions on grammar and literature

a. Although there are numerous examples in the works of Shakespeare and other authors, putting the word 'from' before what six-letter adverb is often cited as a solecism, because its meaning is already 'from what place'?

b. 'He got a good estate by merchandise, and leaving off his trade, lived afterwards at York; from whence he had married my mother.' This sentence forms part of the opening lines of which novel of 1719?

c. 'I will lift up mine eyes unto the hills, from whence cometh my help.' In which book of the Old Testament do these words appear?

4 Ahead of Ontario and the US state of Vermont, which Canadian province is the world's largest producer of maple syrup, with around seventy per cent of the world's total?

Three bonus questions on a European capital

a. Which European capital gave its name, in part, to the settlement that was captured by Britain in 1664 and renamed New York?

b. At a similar latitude to Cape Town and Melbourne, the volcanic Amsterdam Island is inhabited only by scientists. In which ocean is it, and which country has sovereignty?

c. First published in 1998, the Booker prize-winning novel *Amsterdam* is by which author?

5 Scaphopoda, gastropoda and bivalvia are among orders in which animal phylum?

Three bonus questions on art and astronomy

a. 'That man am I, by whose accomplishment / the painter's art was raised from the dead.' These words are from a memorial to which Italian artist, born around 1266?

b. A space probe named after Giotto was part of an 'armada' of craft that made observations of which astronomical object in 1986?

c. A heavenly object generally thought to be Halley's Comet appears in a fresco by Giotto in the Arena Chapel in Padua depicting what event in the early life of Jesus?

6 'Spoon', 'direct-pull', 'roller lever' and 'coaster' are among types of what mechanism, found on bicycles?

Three bonus questions on idioms

a. *Das kommt mir spanisch vor* is a German idiom most nearly approximate to which English equivalent?

b. Which two-word English phrase, suggestive of a European relative, is synonymous with a candid but benevolent adviser or critic?

c. What is the English equivalent of the French idiom *filer a l'Anglais*?

7 Born near Paris in 1862, which composer's works include a book of preludes for piano, the opera *Pelléas and Mélisande*, and the orchestral piece *La Mer*?

Three bonus questions on prominent people who give their names to stations of the Paris Métro. In each case, name the person from the description.

a. Nicknamed 'the Tiger', the prime minister of France who presided at the Paris peace conference in 1919?

b. A socialist leader assassinated in 1914; he was a co-founder of the newspaper *L'Humanité*?

c. The thirty-second president of the United States of America?

8 Answer as soon as your name is called. Meaning 'unwelcome departure from the norm', give the dictionary spelling of the word 'aberration'.

Three bonus questions on the 'color of the year', in the wisdom of the US design corporation Pantone

a. Pantone's 2011 'color of the year' shared its name with which climbing garden plant of the genus *Lonicera*, noted for its intense fragrance?

b. What was Pantone's 2012 'color of the year'? Its two-word alliterative name comprises those of a citrus fruit named after a North African port, and a ballroom dance that originated in Argentina.

c. What is Pantone's 2013 'color of the year'? It shares its name with a variety of the mineral beryl that is valued as a gemstone.

9 What general category of foodstuffs links: the author of *Queen of the Dormitory* and *Jill's Jolliest Term*; the synth-pop duo Soft Cell; and the rabbit leader in *Watership Down*?

Three bonus questions on the verb 'to be' in European languages

a. The first-person singular present tense of the verb *ser* in Spanish spells the name of which condiment, prominent in East Asia?

b. The third-person singular affirmative present tense of the verb 'to be' in Welsh spells the given name of which prominent US actress, born in 1893?

c. The first-person singular present tense of the verb 'to be' in German spells the name of what receptacle in English?

10 Saaremaa, Bornholm and Gotland are among the islands in which body of water, connected to the North Sea by the straits known as the Kattegat and Skagerrak?

Three bonus questions on Neo-Palladian architecture. In each case, name the English county in which the following are located.

a. Holkham Hall, built by Thomas Coke, Earl of Leicester, from the 1730s?

b. The Palladian bridge in Stowe Landscape Gardens, built in the 1730s for the Temple-Grenville family?

c. Finally, Kedleston Hall, the seat of the Curzon family?

11 What intentional feature of Laurence Sterne's *Tristram Shandy* also appears in both *The Collected Works of Billy the Kid* by Michael Ondaatje, and the autobiography of the footballer Len Shackleton, in a chapter entitled 'The Average Director's Knowledge of Football'?

Three bonus questions on the King James Bible. In each case, identify the book of the Old Testament from verses taken from its opening chapter.

a. 'Behold, thou art fair, my love; / Behold, thou art fair; / Thou hast doves' eyes.'

b. 'Moses my servant is dead; now therefore arise, go over this Jordan, thou, and all this people, unto the land which I do give to them, even to the children of Israel.'

   c.   'Blessed is the man that walketh not in the counsel of
        the ungodly, / Nor standeth in the way of sinners, /
        Nor sitteth in the seat of the scornful.'

12 What name is given to the large square cushion covered
    in red cloth that acts as the seat of the Lord Speaker in
    the House of Lords?

Three bonus questions on political theory

   a.   To what was George Orwell referring when he wrote in
        1937 that to the ordinary working man it meant little
        more than 'better wages and shorter hours and nobody
        bossing you about'?

   b.   The term 'Socialism' was first used in France in the early
        1830s by followers of which key figure in Utopianism?
        His major work was *Nouveau Christianisme*.

   c.   Which British Utopian Socialist put his ideas into
        practice when he founded the model industrial
        community of New Lanark in Scotland in 1800?

13 Which animals do battle with mice in
    Batrachomyomachia, the burlesque Greek epic of the
    fifth century BC, once believed to have been written
    by Homer?

Three bonus questions on ancient Greece and Rome

   a.   In ancient Rome, a triclinium was a dining room that
        included three of what item of furniture?

   b.   In classical architecture, what name, meaning 'thrice
        carved', is given to the slightly raised blocks that
        alternate with the metopes in a Doric frieze?

   c.   In the late Roman republic, the first triumvirate was
        an unofficial coalition of Julius Caesar and which
        two figures?

14 A former East India Company clerk elected to the House of Commons in 1865, which philosopher and economist's works include *A System of Logic*, *The Subjection of Women* and *On Liberty*?

Three bonus questions on the films of Stanley Kubrick

a. The 1957 film *Paths of Glory* was based on a novel by Humphrey Cobb which took its title from an elegy of 1751 by which English poet?

b. Which film of 1975 by Stanley Kubrick is based on a novel by Thackeray about the life and exploits of an eighteenth-century Irish adventurer?

c. Born in 1862, the Austrian author Arthur Schnitzler's short story 'Traum-Novelle', or 'Dream Story', was the basis for which film, the last Kubrick completed before his death?

15 Deriving its name from the Greek word for 'being', which branch of metaphysics concerns itself with the philosophical study of existence?

Three bonus questions on rugby players

a. Having played for his national rugby team at under-21 level, who earned the first Best Actor Oscar nomination for a Spanish national with his role in *Before Night Falls*? He won an Academy Award in 2008 for his role in *No Country for Old Men*.

b. Having founded the rugby magazine *Tackle* in 1951, which future revolutionary played for various Argentinian rugby clubs while studying to be a doctor?

c. A former international rugby player for Belgium, Jacques Rogge joined which organisation in 1991, and became its president in 2001?

16 Riefler, Von Sterneck, compensated, torsion and Foucault are varieties of what oscillatory device?

Three bonus questions on two-letter words said to be familiar to serious Scrabble players. In each case, spell the word from its definition.

a. From the Hawaiian language, and worth two points, a word denoting a basaltic lava forming very rough, jagged masses with a light frothy texture?

b. Also worth two points, a Chinese unit of distance, equal to about 600 metres?

c. Worth eleven points, the circulating life force whose existence and properties form a basis for Chinese philosophy and medicine?

17 Answer as soon as your name is called. In binary, a 1 followed by five 1s represents what number in decimal?

Three bonus questions on mathematics, taking a two-by-two matrix with top row 2, 1, and bottom row 1, 2

a. Which eigenvalue of this matrix corresponds to the eigenvector 1, 1?

b. What is the remaining eigenvalue of this matrix, not equal to 3?

c. What is the determinant of this matrix?

18 In physics, what term describes a collision between two objects where the relative speed of approach before the collision and the relative speed of recession afterwards are the same?

Three bonus questions on British libraries

a. The Mitchell Library, one of the largest public reference libraries in Europe, is in which British city?

b. The London Library, the world's largest independent lending library, was founded in 1841 largely due to the efforts of which Scottish historian and biographer?

c. In which city are the John Rylands University Library, the Portico Library and Chetham's Library, the latter being the oldest public library in the English-speaking world?

19 Listen carefully. John Donne's 'Meditation XVII' includes a sentence that begins 'No man is an island'. Which five words, later used by Hemingway as the title of a novel, appear towards the end of this sentence?

Three bonus questions on northern England

a. At an altitude of 893 metres, what is the highest point on the Pennine Way and the highest in England outside the Lake District?

b. The western slopes of Cross Fell are the source of which strong wind, occurring particularly during the spring?

c. Rising near the summit of Cross Fell, which river flows east for more than 80 miles and reaches the North Sea south of Hartlepool?

20 In probability theory, what is the co-variance between two independent real-valued random variables?

Three bonus questions on statistical distributions

a. If x, y and z are independent random variables, each normally distributed with mean 0 and variance 1, then x plus y plus z is also normally distributed with mean 0, and what variance?

b. If x is normally distributed with mean 0 and variance 1, then x2 has what distribution, with 1 degree of freedom?

c. The chi-squared distribution is a special case of a family of distributions that bears the name of which other Greek letter?

21 Highlighting the number of stabbings in Shakespeare, 'Mrs Schofield's GCSE' is a response by which poet to the removal of another of her works from a GCSE syllabus because it was thought to glorify knife crime?

Three bonus questions on art

a. 'With our James, vulgarity begins at home, and should be allowed to stay there.' These words of Oscar Wilde refer to which US artist, born in 1834?

b. Whistler was influenced by which genre of Japanese wood-block prints, whose name translates as 'Pictures of the floating world'?

c. Born in 1760, which artist of the Ukiyo-e school is particularly famous for his *One Hundred Views of Mount Fuji*?

22 Often described as the first British feminist theorist, who examined women's subordination in society in her 1792 work *A Vindication of the Rights of Women*? She died eleven days after giving birth to the future author of *Frankenstein*.

Three bonus questions on a shared name

a. In the Bible, which nephew of Abraham settled in the city of Sodom, from which he fled with his wife during its destruction?

b. In Arthurian legend, which knight was the son of King Lot of Orkney? His adventures included an encounter with the Green Knight.

c. The River Lot rises in the Cévennes and flows for almost 500 kilometres before joining which river?

23 Answer as soon as your name is called. If standard gravity is 10 metres per second squared, and atmospheric pressure is 100,000 pascals, what depth of water corresponds to 1 atmosphere of pressure?

Three bonus questions on a chemical process

a. The chemist Fritz Haber won the Nobel Prize in 1918 for his method of synthesising which compound gas from hydrogen and nitrogen?

b. Haber's method is often named after him and which industrial chemist, who translated it into a large-scale, high-pressure process?

c. The Haber process initially used as a catalyst either uranium or which rare, dense platinum metal?

24 In linguistics, which adjective describes languages in which grammatical structure is expressed largely by inflections rather than by word order? In more general speech, it describes manmade substances that imitate natural products.

Three bonus questions on linguistics

a. In orthography, what Greek-derived term denotes a combination of two letters representing a single sound? An example is the 'c.h.' in the phrase 'chattanooga choo-choo'.

b. What digraph is often used when transliterating the voiced palato-alveolar fricative from Slavic languages, for example in the surname of the leader of the USSR from 1964 to 1982, or the title character of a novel by Pasternak?

c. What digraph is most commonly used in English to represent voiced and voiceless inter-dental fricatives?

25 The letters N.S.S. stand for which pressure group? Founded by Charles Bradlaugh in 1866, it describes itself on its website as 'challenging religious privilege'.

Three bonus questions on tri-junctions or tri-points, in other words, places where three geographical boundaries meet

a. The hill known as the Vaalserberg lies close to the point where the border of Germany meets that separating which two other countries?

b. Giving its name to an agreement of 1985 aimed at simplifying border controls, the town of Schengen lies close to the tri-point of which three countries?

c. Which major city lies immediately to the south of the tri-junction of Germany, France and Switzerland?

26 In a 1954 book on 'the nature of' the eponymous subject, what did the US psychologist Gordon W. Allport describe as 'a feeling, favourable or unfavourable, toward a person or thing, prior to, or not based on, actual experience'?

Three bonus questions on a royal appointment

a. During the reign of Charles I, Nicholas Lanier became the first person appointed to which largely ceremonial position, responsible for composing or performing music for state occasions?

b. Who was appointed Master of the King's Music in 1942? His works include the tone poem 'Tintagel' and the score for the 1948 film *Oliver Twist*.

c. The opera *The Lighthouse* is a work by which composer, appointed Master of the Queen's Music in 2004?

27 Noted for significant contributions in the 1920s to the study of long-term fluctuations, which Russian economist, born in 1892, gives his name to a business cycle of very long duration?

Three bonus questions on invasions of Britain

a. Who was the Roman emperor at the time of the invasion of Britain in AD 43?

b. Commemorated in an Anglo-Saxon poem, which town in Essex was the site of an invasion by Danish forces in the year 991?

c. Which port in west Wales was the site of an abortive French invasion in 1797?

28 Quote: 'The author of this sick little play ... has the traditional, irrational hatred of the police common to all narrow-minded left-wingers and so I shall, no doubt, be the unwilling butt of endless anti-authoritarian jibes.' These words of Inspector Bertozzo appear at the beginning of which farce, first performed in 1970?

Three questions on twentieth-century novels

a. What is the title of the semi-autobiographical novel written by Sylvia Plath and published in 1963, shortly before her death, under the pseudonym Victoria Lucas?

b. *Of Human Bondage*, published in 1915, is a semi-autobiographical novel by which novelist and playwright?

c. Which US author wrote the semi-autobiographical novel *The Dharma Bums*, published in 1958, a year after the novel for which he is best known?

29 What is the only country that is a member of both the G20 and the Arab League?

Three bonus questions on geography

a. The cities of Rouen and Le Havre are in which French *département*? The two words of its name denote a major river and proximity to the sea, both in French and English.

b. Associated with Chagall and Matisse, which major city is the prefecture of the Alpes-Maritimes *département*?

c. Its two-word name denoting a river and a body of water, which *département* in Brittany has Nantes as its prefecture?

30 What four-letter prefix links: the name of the layer of the Earth's atmosphere between the stratosphere and the thermosphere; the land lying between the Tigris and Euphrates rivers; and the geological era that includes the Triassic and Cretaceous periods?

Three bonus questions on geology

a. What name is given to the assumption that natural processes and laws currently operating have always operated in the same way in the past, and are valid everywhere?

b. Born in 1726, which Scottish geologist identified sites such as Siccar Point in Berwickshire as 'unconformities' which provided proof of the Uniformitarian Theory of Geological Change? His work was later popularised by Charles Lyell.

c. What term is used for the contrasting idea that geological change on Earth has been driven by sudden, large-scale violent occurrences?

'I watched *University Challenge* as a kid, and I didn't really understand what a student was; the only time you encountered students on British television was on *Brideshead Revisited*, and *University Challenge* was the flip-side of that – there were people with regional accents, and it seemed much more democratic.'

DAVID NICHOLLS
Author, *Starter for Ten*

The Answers

1 (Edouard) Manet (*Manet and the Post-Impressionists*)
   a.   Scapula / shoulder blade
   b.   Humerus
   c.   Clavicle / collar bone

2 Hopping
   a.   Night time / darkness
   b.   Vitamin A / retinol
   c.   Plants that flower at night

3 *A Midsummer Night's Dream*
   a.   Whence
   b.   *Robinson Crusoe*
   c.   Psalms (number 121)

4 Quebec
   a.   Amsterdam
   b.   Indian Ocean; France (part of the French Southern and Antarctic Lands)
   c.   Ian McEwan

5 Mollusca / molluscs
   a.   Giotto (di Bondone)
   b.   Halley's Comet
   c.   The Adoration of the Magi

6 Brakes

    a. That's (all) Greek to me (accept similar; the phrase roughly translates as 'that seems Spanish to me')
    b. Dutch uncle
    c. To take French leave

7 (Claude) Debussy
    a. Clemenceau (Georges Clemenceau, 1841–1929; the station is Champs-Élysees – Clemenceau)
    b. (Jean) Jaurès (1859–1914)
    c. Franklin D. Roosevelt

8 A.b.e.r.r.a.t.i.o.n.
    a. Honeysuckle
    b. Tangerine tango
    c. Emerald

9 Nuts (Angela Brazil, Marc Almond, Hazel)
    a. Soy (as in soy sauce; NB there are two verbs 'to be' in Spanish: ser and estar, hence the specification)
    b. Mae West
    c. Bin

10 Baltic (Sea)
    a. Norfolk
    b. Buckinghamshire
    c. Derbyshire

11 Blank page(s)
    a. Song of Solomon
    b. Joshua
    c. Psalms

12 Woolsack
    a. Socialism (in *The Road to Wigan Pier*)
    b. (Claude-Henri de Rouvroy), Saint-Simon (1760–1825)
    c. Robert Owen (1771–1858)

13 Frogs
- **a.** Couch
- **b.** Triglyphs
- **c.** Pompey (Gnaeus Pompeius Magnus) and Crassus (Marcus Licinius Crassus)

14 John Stuart Mill
- **a.** (Thomas) Gray
- **b.** *Barry Lyndon*
- **c.** *Eyes Wide Shut*

15 Ontology
- **a.** Javier Bardem
- **b.** 'Che' (Ernesto) Guevara
- **c.** International Olympic Committee / IOC

16 Pendulum
- **a.** Aa
- **b.** Li
- **c.** Qi

17 63 (32+16+8+4+2+1, or 2 to the 6 minus 1)
- **a.** 3 (working: (1,1) x matrix = (3, 3) = 3 x (1,1))
- **b.** 1 (working: (1, -1) x matrix = (1, -1) = 1 x (1, -1))
- **c.** 3 (working: the determinant of the matrix is equal to ad – bc, and 2x2 – 1x1 = 3)

18 Elastic (collision)
- **a.** Glasgow (founded after a bequest by tobacco magnate Stephen Mitchell, 1789–1874)
- **b.** (Thomas) Carlyle
- **c.** Manchester

19 'For whom the bell tolls'
- **a.** Cross Fell
- **b.** The Helm Wind

    c.   Tees

20 o (Working: $cov(x,y) = e(xy) - e(x)e(y)$. If x and y are independent then $e(xy) = e(x)e(y)$)
    a.   3
    b.   Chi-squared (distribution)
    c.   Gamma

21 Carol Ann Duffy (supposedly, an exam invigilator of that name lodged the initial complaint about 'Education for Leisure')
    a.   (James Abbott McNeill) Whistler
    b.   Ukiyo-e
    c.   (Katsushika) Hokusai

22 Mary Wollstonecraft (She married William Godwin in 1797; her daughter was Mary Wollstonecraft Godwin, later Shelley, of course.)
    a.   Lot
    b.   Sir Gawain
    c.   Garonne

23 Ten metres
    a.   Ammonia
    b.   (Carl) Bosch
    c.   Osmium

24 Synthetic
    a.   Digraph (not diphthong, which refers to two adjacent, different vowel sounds within the same syllable)
    b.   Z.h. (prompt for the letters, not the sound; Brezhnev and Zhivago, of course)
    c.   T.h. (prompt for the letters, not the sound)

25 National Secular Society
    a.   Belgium and the Netherlands (accept Holland)
    b.   Germany, France and Luxembourg
    c.   Basel / Basle

26 Prejudice
- **a.** Master of the King's Musick
- **b.** (Sir Arnold) Bax
- **c.** (Sir Peter) Maxwell Davies

27 (Nikolai) Kondratiev (1892–1938; the Kondratiev wave)
- **a.** Claudius
- **b.** Maldon (the poem is 'The Battle of Maldon')
- **c.** Fishguard (accept Abergwaun)

28 *Accidental Death of an Anarchist* (by Dario Fo)
- **a.** *The Bell Jar*
- **b.** (W. Somerset) Maugham
- **c.** Jack Kerouac

29 Saudi Arabia
- **a.** Seine-Maritime
- **b.** Nice
- **c.** Loire-Atlantique

30 Meso- (mesosphere, Mesopotamia, Mesozoic)
- **a.** Uniformitarianism (accept Gradualism)
- **b.** (James) Hutton (1726–1797; Charles Lyell, 1797–1875)
- **c.** Catastrophism

Match Three

1 Known as the Kelvin Wedge, the angle enclosed by the wake of a vessel travelling in deep water is theoretically constant regardless of the velocity of the vessel. To within five degrees, what is the numerical value of this angle?

Three bonus questions on crystal structures in chemistry

a. Which element was discovered by the Curies in 1898, some months before their discovery of radium? It has two metallic allotropes; the alpha form is an example of a simple cubic structure, and the beta form is rhombohedral.

b. There are two crystal lattices in which hard spheres can be packed to fill space as efficiently as possible. One lattice is the hexagon close packed, or h.c.p.; what is the other?

c. In a sodium chloride crystal, how many sodium ions surround a chloride ion as nearest neighbour?

2 The site of a major volcanic eruption in 1997, Chances Peak in the Soufriere Hills is on which island, a British Overseas Territory in the Caribbean Sea?

Three bonus questions on the works of John Masefield. In each case, identify the poems in which the following lines appear.

a. 'Quinquireme of Nineveh from distant Ophir / Rowing home to haven in sunny Palestine...'

b. 'Out into street I ran uproarious / The devil dancing in me glorious...'

c. 'And all I ask is a tall ship and a star to steer her by...'

3 Answer as soon as your name is called. What number results when you multiply the numbers in the titles of the first and second albums by Adele, released in 2008 and 2011?

Three bonus questions on herbs and spices

a. Its seeds forming in three-sided pods, which member of the ginger family gives its name to a range of hills in south India?

b. Its name derived from the Greek for 'to grind the teeth', which liquorice-like resin is used in an eponymous alcoholic drink similar to ouzo?

c. Which aromatic spice consists of the casing of the nutmeg berry?

4 Operation Jubilee was the codename for the 1942 Anglo-Canadian amphibious raid on which French port?

Three bonus questions on meteorology

a. What quantity is defined as the ratio of the partial pressure of water vapour in the atmosphere to the saturated vapour pressure for a given temperature?

b. What is the name of the instrument used to measure humidity?

c. What precise name is given to the temperature at which the relative humidity is 100 per cent?

5 The VIX Index, or the Chicago Board Options Exchange Volatility Index, is a widely used measure of risk and market volatility sometimes known by what descriptive term, used by Robert Harris as the title of his 2011 novel about trading in the financial markets?

Three bonus questions on geology

a. Which geological era is subdivided into periods that include the Triassic and Jurassic?

b. Also known as the K.T. Event, the Cretaceous-Paleogene extinction event at the end of the Mesozoic period eliminated around 80 per cent of animal species. How many million years ago did this occur? You may have 5 million either way.

c. If, in the Mesozoic era, one set sail from the Laurasian supercontinent across the Tethys Sea, on which supercontinent would one eventually land?

6 Whose grave is marked by a tombstone placed behind protective glass by the Irish government to prevent it from 'lipstick erosion' caused by the number of people kissing it? It was designed by Jacob Epstein and lies in Père Lachaise Cemetery in Paris.

Three bonus questions on medical terminology. In each case, give the anatomical features denoted by the following prefixes.

a. Cheiro-?

b. Stetho-?

c. Rhino-?

7 Richard Wagner was inspired to create which opera of 1843 by his experience four years earlier of a dangerous sea crossing from Riga to London?

Three bonus questions on composers born during the 1860s. In each case, name the composer from their listed works.

a. *The Karelia Suite*, *The Swan of Tuonela* and the tone poem *Tapiola*?

b. The French composer whose austere piano pieces include the *Gymnopédies* and *Gnossiennes*?

c. The German composer of operas including *Ariadne auf Naxos* and *Der Rosenkavalier*?

8 Living in exile during the reign of Mary I, who became Elizabeth I's Secretary of State in 1573, and was known as the Queen's Chief Spymaster?

Three bonus questions on kings and queens

a. Widow of the Duke of Brittany, Joan of Navarre married which English king four years after he seized the throne? The mother of eight children by her first marriage, she outlived him and his son and successor.

b. Joan, sometimes known as 'the Fair Maid of Kent', was the mother of Henry's predecessor, Richard II. Which royal figure, who died in 1376, was his father?

c. Joan Beaufort, daughter of the Earl of Somerset, married which Scottish king in 1424?

9 Which year saw the birth of Lewis Carroll, the death of Goethe, the end of the Greek War of Independence, the foundation of the University of Durham, and the passing of the Great Reform Act?

Three bonus questions on authors. In each case, the surname of the first person described is the given name of the second, for example 'C.S. Lewis' and 'Lewis Carroll'. Your answer must include the given name and surname of both people described.

   a. A US zoologist and author of the 1963 work *Silent Spring*, and the Southern Gothic novelist whose works include *The Heart Is a Lonely Hunter* and *The Ballad of the Sad Café*?

   b. Two US novelists: the author of *The Jungle*, born in 1878, and the author of *Main Street* and *Elmer Gantry*, born in 1885?

   c. Both born in 1935, the authors perhaps best known for *The White Hotel* and *Schindler's Ark* respectively?

10 Not to be confused with a river in Kent, which atoll in the central Pacific gives its name to a battle of June 1942 that is often described as a turning point in the Pacific War?

Three bonus questions on physics

   a. Diurnal, semi-diurnal and mixed are different local manifestations of what phenomenon, whose cause was first correctly explained by Isaac Newton in his *Principia Mathematica* of 1687?

   b. As a residual gravitational effect, the tidal force exerted on the Earth by a distant body depends inversely on approximately what power of the distance?

   c. What specific four-letter term describes the tides of smallest range, occurring at intermediate phases of the Moon?

11 The words 'horse' and 'Spanish' may precede which word to form the common names of two unrelated trees?

Three bonus questions on surnames and their anagrams. In each case, give *both* words or names from the explanation or definition.

a. 'Generalissimo and head of nationalist China from 1928 until his death in 1975', and 'being in persistent dull pain, for example, of the head or teeth'?

b. 'Irene, described as "a well-known adventuress" in the Sherlock Holmes story "A Scandal in Bohemia"', and '*Alnus glutinosa*, a native British tree of the birch family'?

c. 'Author of *The Little Mermaid*', and 'entangled or caught in a trap'?

12 In George Orwell's *Nineteen Eighty-Four*, two of the Party's slogans are 'War is Peace' and 'Freedom is Slavery'. What is the third?

Three bonus questions on place names in Turkish

a. In Turkish, Bulgaria is Bulgaristan, and Armenia is Ermenistan. Which of Turkey's neighbours is known as Yunanistan?

b. Which European country is known in Turkish as Karadag, meaning 'Black Mountain'?

c. Macaristan is the Turkish name of which EU member state?

13 In the children's book by J. Otto Seibold and Vivian Walsh, 'Olive the Other Reindeer' is actually what sort of animal?

Three bonus questions on famous Belgians, as commemorated in the names of stations on the Brussels Metro

   a. The Belgian prime minister from 1918 to 1920? He shares a surname with the French Romantic artist who painted *Liberty Leading the People*.

   b. An architect of the Art Nouveau style whose chief works include the Maison du Peuple and the Hotel Solvay, both in Brussels?

   c. The cyclist who won the Tour de France five times between 1969 and 1974?

14 Answer as soon as your name is called. What is the smallest prime divisor of the number 2013?

Three bonus questions on astronomy

   a. Which French astronomer, born in 1730, gives his name to the list of astronomical objects designed to help distinguish between permanent objects in the sky and transient ones, such as comets?

   b. Messier 110 is the latest addition to the catalogue, included in 1967 after it had been found as a bright satellite of which large spiral galaxy, the nearest such neighbour of the Milky Way?

   c. Added in 1953, M108 can be observed as an edge-on spiral galaxy near to Beta Ursae Majoris, a 'pointer star' traditionally known by what name?

15 Born in 1837, which Dutch physicist gives his name to the bond or forces caused by the interactions of electric dipole moments in atoms and molecules?

Three bonus questions on the actor Rupert Graves

a. Early in his career, Rupert Graves played Freddy Honeychurch and Alec Scudder in Merchant-Ivory dramatisations of novels by which author?

b. Graves plays Dominic Stone in which 2005 film, based on a graphic novel by Alan Moore and David Lloyd?

c. Appearing frequently in Conan Doyle's stories, which character does Graves play in the TV series *Sherlock*?

16 The 'Singing Cowboy' Gene Autry followed his 1949 single success 'Rudolph the Red-Nosed Reindeer' with a song in 1950 about which other seasonal figure?

Three bonus questions on tea production in West Asia

a. Producing mainly for the domestic market, Rize Province is a major tea-growing area in which West Asian country, one of the world's largest producers of tea?

b. Tea accounts for around 20 per cent of the agricultural output of which country on the Black Sea? It produced a large proportion of the tea in the former USSR.

c. The provinces of Gilan and Mazandran, south of the Caspian Sea, are tea-growing areas in which country?

17 Kate Bush's *Words for Snow* in 2011, Paul Simon's 'Ways to Leave Your Lover' in 1975, and E.L. James's *Shades of Grey* in 2012 are linked by what two-digit number?

Three bonus questions on memory

a. *Moonwalking with Einstein: The Art and Science of Remembering Everything* recounts which journalist's experience of winning the US Memory Championships after just one year of training?

b. Its invention traditionally ascribed to the Greek poet Simonides of Ceos, what two-word term denotes the mnemonic device also known as 'the method of loci', employed by the fictional Hannibal Lecter among others?

c. In a study of 2000 at University College London, the right posterior hippocampus, the brain area involved in spatial navigation, was found to be significantly larger than normal in people with which job?

18 'Then arrowroot, cocoa and biscuit hoosh sweetened; then a plum pudding; then cocoa with raisins, and finally a dessert of caramels and ginger.' In whose diary of 1911 does this description of a Christmas Day meal appear? It began with a helping of horsemeat flavoured with onion and curry powder.

Three bonus questions on the stage works of George Bernard Shaw

a. Described as 'a paradoxical version of the Don Juan story', in which play by Shaw is John Tanner pursued by Ann Whitefield?

b. *In the Beginning: B.C. 4004* and *As Far as Thought Can Reach: A.D. 31,920* are the first and last in which series of five plays by Shaw?

c. Which play by Shaw examines the conflict between a Salvation Army officer and her father, a wealthy armaments manufacturer?

19 Answer as soon as your name is called. Give the dictionary spelling of the unsegmented gliding speech sound known as a 'diphthong'.

Three bonus questions on German-born people with the earliest birthdates in the International Movie Database (IMDB)

a. Featured on the soundtrack of the film *A Beautiful Mind*, the twelfth-century choral work 'Columba Aspexit' is a Sequence for St Maximinus composed by which German abbess, known as the 'Sybil of the Rhine'?

b. Born in Nuremberg in 1571, which artist was given an art department credit on the 1950s German animated series *Our Sandman*?

c. Both *The Simpsons* and the Michael Haneke film *The White Ribbon* have featured the 1529 hymn 'A Mighty Fortress Is Our God', the work of which religious reformer?

20 A useful tool for teaching algebraic group theory, which puzzle toy was marketed from 1977 by Konsumex, Hungary's state trading company, having been developed from a prototype made of 27 wooden blocks?

Three bonus questions on wealth and riches

a. 'The chief enjoyment of riches consists in the parade of riches.' Which Scottish economist wrote these words in a work of 1776?

b. 'To be clever enough to get all that money, one must be stupid enough to want it.' Who wrote these words in *The Wisdom of Father Brown*?

c. Give the word that completes this remark, which has been attributed to L. Ron Hubbard: 'If you really want to make a million ... the quickest way is to start your own ...' what?

21 What six-letter adjective links the nicknames of the snowboarder Shaun White and several Finnish sportsmen, including Matti Nykanen and Paavo Nurmi, with a novel by Erica Jong and a British comedy team that made its television debut in 1969?

Three bonus questions on military awards

a. Preceding the Victoria Cross by two years, which medal was instituted in 1854 to recognise acts of outstanding courage by other ranks during the Crimean War?

b. In 1855, the Royal Navy introduced which equivalent to the DCM, represented by the abbreviation CGM?

c. Which late-medieval order of chivalry was revived by George I as a regular military order, and was expanded and divided into two classes, military and civil, by the Prince Regent in 1815?

22 What two colours link the flags of Shetland, Somalia, Martinique, South Carolina, Tenerife, Finland and Greece?

Three bonus questions on the US Ivy League universities

a. Which Ivy League institution was founded in Hanover, New Hampshire, in 1769, one of its original goals being the education of Native Americans?

b. One of the oldest colleges in the USA, which Ivy League university was founded in 1764 as the College of Rhode Island?

c. Founded in 1865 in Ithaca, New York, which is the youngest Ivy League institution?

23 What ascending sequence of numbers links Schumann's 'Spring' symphony, Mahler's 'Resurrection' and Beethoven's 'Eroica'?

Three bonus questions on the Shipping Forecast

a. The Shipping Forecast areas of North Utsire and South Utsire lie off the west coast of which country?

b. Ronaldsway lies in which Shipping Forecast area, bounded by Malin to the north and Lundy to the south?

c. Which area lies between south-east Iceland and Fair Isle, and contains the group of islands after which it is named?

24 'He lived a brief, passionate, unhappy life. He wrote magnificent poetry. And he introduced a new word for "kiss" into the European languages.' These words of the classicist Gilbert Highet refer to which Roman poet of the first century BC?

Three bonus questions on writers on gardening

a. Which poet and novelist wrote a weekly gardening column for *The Observer* from 1947, and is also noted for restoring the gardens at Sissinghurst Castle in the 1930s?

b. Which artist and designer wrote prolifically on gardening between 1881 and 1932? Some of her best-known garden designs were in collaboration with Edward Lutyens.

c. 'Rose Blight' was the pseudonym used by which academic and literary figure for her gardening column in *Private Eye* in the 1970s?

25 Answer as soon as you buzz. A university term begins on 22 September. After this day, how many days remain until the end of the calendar year?

Three bonus questions on years

    a. What multiple of three is the year in which Henry VIII came to the throne?

    b. What multiple of four is the year in which Edward VIII abdicated?

    c. Which English king came to the throne in August of the year whose factors include 3, 5, 99 and 297?

26 Give a complete answer as soon as your name is called. In addition to alpha and omega, five Greek letters have names that are five-letter words ending in 'a'. For ten points, give me four of them.

Three bonus questions on squirrels in literature

    a. In *Romeo and Juliet*, which supernatural figure is described as 'the fairies' midwife', whose chariot is 'an empty hazel-nut / made by the joiner squirrel'?

    b. Which historical figure wrote an epigraph in 1772 on the death of a pet squirrel, Mungo, given by him as a gift to the young daughter of friends whilst on a diplomatic journey from the Colonies to Great Britain?

    c. 'Policemen, like red squirrels, must be protected.' These words appear in the 1967 play *Loot* by which dramatist, who died the same year?

27 Which French film director's work includes what is often described as the first science fiction film? Released in 1902, it features a sequence in which a space rocket lands in the eye of the Man in the Moon.

Three bonus questions on early film-makers

a. Born in Bristol in 1855, which film-maker developed an early film camera said to be capable of taking ten pictures per second? He is the subject of the 1951 biographical drama *The Magic Box*.

b. Described as 'the film equivalent of the discovery of Tutankhamen's tomb', around 800 reels of negatives rediscovered in Blackburn in 1994 were produced by which pair of film-makers?

c. Which French brothers created the cinématographe moving-picture system in the late nineteenth century?

28 What term denotes the paraphyletic group of non-vascular land plants that includes mosses, liverworts and hornworts?

Three bonus questions on occupational diseases

a. What two-word name was commonly given to phosphonecrosis, a disease once prevalent in workers in match factories and caused by exposure to high levels of phosphorus?

b. Byssinosis is a respiratory disorder particularly common in workers inhaling dust particles produced by which crop?

c. What two-word name is given to coalworkers' pneumoconiosis because of the visible effect of coal dust on the respiratory system?

29 What is the common name of fish of the genus *Anguilla*? The Sargasso Sea, south of Bermuda, is a major breeding ground; larvae then grow and migrate to rivers in Europe and North America.

Three bonus questions on psychology

a. After the Roman goddess of the Moon, what is the name of the complex in which a woman has a repressed desire to become a man?

b. A complex in psychology that relates to an impulsive desire of a man to kill his mother is named after which figure in Greek mythology? The son of Agamemnon, he murders his mother, Clytemnestra?

c. Which complex in psychology is described by the Austrian psychiatrist Alfred Adler in *The Neurotic Constitution* as 'a compensation in the sense of an enhancement of the self-esteem'?

30 Pontus Euxinus was a name given by the ancients to which inland body of water?

Three bonus questions on geography

a. What three-word term denotes the large expanse of sea that lies immediately south of the Nullarbor Plain? It is sometimes defined as extending from Cape Pasley to Cape Carnot, a distance of more than 1,000 kilometres.

b. Sharing its name with a country, which Bight occupies the part of the Gulf of Guinea formerly known as the Slave Coast?

c. Which Bight is the modern name of the Shipping Forecast area formerly known as Heligoland?

The Answers

1 39 degrees (so accept 34–44 degrees)
    a. Polonium
    b. Cubic close packed / c.c.c. (accept face centred cubic / f.c.c.)
    c. 6

2 Montserrat
    a. 'Cargoes'
    b. 'The Everlasting Mercy'
    c. 'Sea Fever'

3 399 (i.e. 19 x 21)
    a. Cardamom
    b. Mastic
    c. Mace

4 Dieppe
    a. Relative humidity (do not accept only humidity or absolute humidity)
    b. Hygrometer (not hydrometer, which measures the specific gravity or relative density of liquids)
    c. The dew point

5 (The) Fear Index
    a. Mesozoic
    b. 65.5 (so accept 60.5–70.5)
    c. Gondwanaland / Gondwana

6 Oscar Wilde (protected by glass in November 2011)
- **a.** Hand
- **b.** Chest
- **c.** Nose

7 *The Flying Dutchman / Der Fliegende Hollander*
- **a.** (Jean) Sibelius (1865–1957)
- **b.** (Erik) Satie (1866–1925; Debussy was born during the same decade)
- **c.** Richard Strauss (need both names, of course)

8 (Sir Francis) Walsingham (1532–1590)
- **a.** Henry IV
- **b.** Edward, Prince of Wales / the Black Prince (aka Edward of Woodstock, eldest son of Edward III and older brother of John of Gaunt who was Henry IV's father)
- **c.** James I

9 1832
- **a.** Rachel Carson and Carson McCullers
- **b.** Upton Sinclair and Sinclair Lewis
- **c.** D.M. Thomas (Donald Michael Thomas) and Thomas Keneally

10 Midway
- **a.** (Equilibrium) Tides
- **b.** The third power / the cube
- **c.** Neap

11 Chestnut (*Castanea vesca* and *Æsculus hippocastanum*)
- **a.** Chiang and aching
- **b.** Adler and alder
- **c.** Andersen and ensnared

12 'Ignorance is Strength'
- **a.** Greece (from 'Ionia')

    b.   Montenegro
    c.   Hungary

13 Dog / canine (a Jack Russell terrier called Olive, who misunderstands the line 'all of [i.e. Olive] the other reindeer...')
    a.   (Léon) Delacroix
    b.   (Victor) Horta (1861–1947)
    c.   Eddy Merckx

14 3 (if the individual digits add up to a multiple of 3, the number itself is divisible by 3)
    a.   (Charles) Messier (Messier's own final list, published in 1781, consisted of 103 objects)
    b.   Andromeda (accept NGC224 / Messier 31 / M31; the Magellanic Clouds are nearer but are not large spiral galaxies; Messier 110 is a dwarf spheroid galaxy)
    c.   Merak (not Dubhe, which is Alpha Ursae Majoris)

15 (Johannes) van der Waals
    a.   E.M. Forster (*A Room with a View* and *Maurice*)
    b.   *V for Vendetta*
    c.   (Detective Inspector Greg) Lestrade

16 'Frosty the Snowman'
    a.   Turkey
    b.   Georgia
    c.   Iran

17 50
    a.   Joshua Foer (brother of *Everything Is Illuminated* author Jonathan Safran Foer)
    b.   Memory palace
    c.   London cab drivers / cabbies / taxi drivers

18 (Captain Robert Falcon) Scott (1868–1912)
    a.   *Man and Superman*

b. *Back to Methuselah*

c. *Major Barbara*

19. D.i.p.h.t.h.o.n.g.

    a. St Hildegard / Hildegard of Bingen

    b. (Albrecht) Dürer

    c. Martin Luther

20. Rubik's Cube

    a. Adam Smith (in *The Wealth of Nations*)

    b. (G.K.) Chesterton

    c. Religion

21. Flying (the Flying Tomato, the Flying Finn, *Fear of Flying*, Monty Python's Flying Circus)

    a. Distinguished Conduct Medal / DCM (not Distinguished Service Order / DSO, which is for commissioned officers)

    b. Conspicuous Gallantry Medal

    c. Order of the Bath

22. Blue and white

    a. Dartmouth (College)

    b. Brown (in Providence)

    c. Cornell

23. 1 – 2 – 3

    a. Norway

    b. The Irish Sea

    c. Faeroes

24. Catullus (*Poets in a Landscape*)

    a. Vita Sackville-West

    b. Gertrude Jekyll

    c. Germaine Greer

25 100 (8 in September, then 31 + 30 + 31)
- **a.** 1509 (3 x 503)
- **b.** 1936 (4 x 484)
- **c.** Henry VII (i.e. 1485)

26 Gamma, delta, theta, kappa, sigma (not beta, zeta, iota or lambda)
- **a.** Queen Mab
- **b.** Benjamin Franklin
- **c.** Joe Orton

27 (Georges) Méliès (*A Trip to the Moon*)
- **a.** (William) Friese-Greene
- **b.** (Sagar) Mitchell and James) Kenyon
- **c.** (Auguste and Louis) Lumière

28 Bryophytes / bryophyte (marchantiophyta refers specifically to liverworts, anthocerotophyta to hornworts)
- **a.** Phossy jaw
- **b.** Cotton
- **c.** Black lung

29 Eels
- **a.** Diana (complex)
- **b.** Orestes
- **c.** Inferiority (complex)

30 The Black Sea
- **a.** Great Australian Bight
- **b.** (Bight of) Benin
- **c.** German Bight

Match Four

1. First serialised in 1890, in which novel does the title character murder the painter Basil Hallward?

Three bonus questions on a play by Shakespeare

  a. Tradition has it that which of Shakespeare's plays was written at the behest of Queen Elizabeth I, who wanted to see a character from the History Plays 'in love'?

  b. In Act 5, Scene 5 of *The Merry Wives of Windsor*, Falstaff is tricked into impersonating which mythological figure, a spirit said to haunt Windsor Forest?

  c. *The Merry Wives of Windsor* was the basis for the opera *Sir John in Love*, first performed in 1929, by which English composer?

2. 'Power expands through the distribution of secrecy.' These are the words of which author, whose works include *The Constant Gardener* and *The Spy Who Came in from the Cold*?

Three bonus questions on a photographer

  a. '[Her work] falls metaphorically between Marlene Dietrich's legs and the bitter lives of migratory potato pickers.' These words of Robert Capa describe which US photographer, who died at the age of 99 in 2012?

b. Eve Arnold was particularly associated with which actress, whom she photographed over a ten-year period, including noteworthy shots on the set of her last film, *The Misfits*?

c. Quote: '[Eve Arnold] photographed four prime ministers. Alec Douglas-Home carried her equipment into the house; Ted Heath went swimming to evade her; and John Major gave her a hug.' Which prime minister, according to the obituary in the *Daily Telegraph*, was 'the only one who told her how to take her pictures'?

3 Which fictional character earned Academy Awards for both the actors who portrayed him on film? The first award, for Best Actor at the 1973 ceremony, was memorably declined. The second, for Best Supporting Actor, was awarded in 1975, for portraying him in his earlier years.

> **Three bonus questions on world currencies, specifically those that in recent years have had a value greater than that of the US dollar. In each case, identify the currency and the country from the three-letter code of the International Standards Organisation.**
>
> **a.** First, for five points: KWD?
>
> **b.** Second: AZN?
>
> **c.** Finally: CHF?

4 What name links: a so-called 'phenomenon' of cell degeneration in humans; a growth model used to value businesses or shares; the British general killed by the forces of the Mahdi in 1885; and an outbreak of anti-Catholic civil disorder in eighteenth-century London?

Three bonus questions on world rulers. I will read a list of rulers who were on the throne or in power during the first year of a century of the Common Era. In each case, I simply want the century.

a. Robert III of Scotland; Charles VI or 'the Well-Beloved' of France; and the Asian conqueror Tamerlane?

b. Raja Raja the Great of the Chola Empire of South India; Boleslav the Valiant of Poland; and Æthelred the Unready of England?

c. Emperor He of the Eastern Han dynasty, Pacorus II of Parthia; and the Roman Emperor Trajan?

5 Focusing mainly on the Battle of Stalingrad, which novel was banned in the USSR and finally published in the west in 1980, sixteen years after the death of its author, Vasily Grossman?

Three bonus questions on ancient and modern Europe

a. Which ancient people did Julius Caesar describe as 'the bravest [of the peoples of Gaul], because they are farthest from the civilisation and refinement of [our] province'? They give their name to a present-day European country.

b. Which nomadic people established their 'first empire' south of the Danube in the late seventh century and adopted the language of the Slavic peoples in the area under their rule? They give their name to a country in south-eastern Europe.

c. Sigobert the Lame and his son Chlodoric the Parricide were among the rulers of which Germanic people, who give their name to a major western European country?

6 'Fitzclarence' was the surname given to the ten illegitimate children born between 1794 and 1807 to the actress Dorothea Jordan and which future king?

Three bonus questions on given names and their anagrams. In each case, give both words from the explanation or definition.

a. The given name of the author of *Nights at the Circus*, and the principle ore of lead?

b. The regnal name of six popes, including one Englishman, and the derived SI unit of plane angle?

c. The king of Wessex who excelled in both rule and scholarship, and a term meaning wider at one end than the other, as of nostrils or trousers?

7 The winner of the 1999 Turner Prize, which British artist made his debut as a feature film director with *Hunger* in 2008, followed in 2011 by *Shame*?

Three bonus questions on an art gallery

a. Established in 1897, the collection of which London gallery includes *The Laughing Cavalier* by Frans Hals and Poussin's *A Dance to the Music of Time*?

b. The Wallace Collection includes a number of works by which artist, active in Paris in the first two decades of the eighteenth century and often credited with the invention of the genre known as *fêtes galantes*?

c. Both in the Wallace Collection, *Perseus and Andromeda* and *The Rape of Europa* are works by which Venetian artist, born around 1488?

8 Home to its country's oldest institution of higher education, which city lies on the Neckar river, around ninety kilometres south of Frankfurt?

Three bonus questions on diseases of the vascular system. In each case, give the term from the description.

a. A localised swelling or widening of an artery, often due to the weakening of its wall?

b. A spasm of pain in the chest, often caused by the inability of the coronary arteries to bring enough oxygen-laden blood to the heart?

c. A Greek-derived term meaning the formation of a blood clot within the blood vessels or heart?

9. The name of which composite nuclear particle containing six quarks forms the first eight letters of a book of the Old Testament?

Three bonus questions on people born on the same day. In each case, identify both people from their works.

a. Both born on 30 November 1874, the authors of *A History of the English-Speaking Peoples* and *Anne of Green Gables*?

b. Both born on 6 May 1856, the authors of *The Interpretation of Dreams* and *The North Pole: Its Discovery in 1909*?

c. Both born on 12 February 1809, the authors of *The Descent of Man* and the short speech known as the Gettysburg Address?

10. Listen carefully. Which positive integer n maximises the expression: 100 minus n, all times n?

Three bonus questions on 'buzzwords' of 2012, according to the Macmillan Online Dictionary

   a.   What term describes the activity of getting a large group of people to finance a particular project, especially by using a website where they can make contributions?

   b.   Usually taking place at an organised event, 'swishing' is the activity of swapping what general type of item with other people?

   c.   What two-word term denotes a proposal in which Scotland would have economic independence from the rest of the UK but would still remain a part of it?

11 Listen carefully and answer as soon as your name is called. A segment of wire has resistance r. If its cross-sectional area is doubled, what is the new value of the wire's resistance?

Three bonus questions on ions

   a.   Which element has the largest first ionisation energy?

   b.   Born in Prague in 1850, which scientist gives his name to the series in which ions are ranked according to their ability to stabilise the structures of proteins?

   c.   The charge of a sodium ion is plus one. What is the charge of a dichromate ion?

12 Introduced in 2011, the upper case 'P-P' logo shown at the start and end of relevant television programmes is a symbol denoting what?

Three bonus questions on shorter words that can be made using any of the letters of the word 'whimsical'. In each case, give the word from the definition.

a. The unstressed, central vowel; for example, the first sound of the word 'again'. In the international phonetic alphabet, it is represented by an inverted lower-case letter 'e'.

b. From the Latin for 'eyelash', minute hair-like projections on the surface of some cells; they are used as a means of locomotion in some aquatic organisms.

c. A computer coding system that assigns numbers to letters, digits and symbols? It is a 7-bit binary code, allowing for 128 characters to be represented.

13 What seven-word utterance by Aneurin Bevan was used as the title of a 1998 album by the Manic Street Preachers?

Three bonus questions on arts festivals

a. First held in 1176 and revived in its present form in 1860, which festival derives its name from the Welsh word for 'sit'?

b. Founded in 1947 by the theatre director Jean Vilar, which French festival's venues include the inner courtyard of the city's Palais de Papes?

c. In late January, the Colombian seaport of Cartagena holds an offshoot of which literary festival?

14 Which Swiss city on the northern shore of Lake Geneva gave its name to a school of economists led by Léon Walras and Vilfredo Pareto? It is also home to the headquarters of the International Olympic Committee.

Three bonus questions on recent works on economics

a. Which US Nobel laureate and former chief economist at the World Bank is the author of *Freefall: Free Markets and the Sinking of the Global Economy*?

b. Sometimes called 'Dr Doom' for his prophetic remarks about the world financial crisis, which Turkish-born US economist co-wrote *Crisis Economics: A Crash Course in the Future of Finance*?

c. Which term completes the title of a 2010 book by the South Korean economist Ha-Joon Chang: *23 Things They Don't Tell You about* ... what?

15 Formed at Netscape in 1998 as an open source project, which global non-profit organisation created the Firefox web browser?

Three bonus questions on antibacterial agents

a. The bacterial synthesis of which vitamin is inhibited by sulphonamides?

b. What bacterial process is blocked by aminoglycoside antibiotics such as streptomycin?

c. What structural component of gram-positive bacterial cells is targeted by penicillins and cephalosporins?

16 According to Kepler's third law, the period of a planetary orbit is proportional to what power of the length of the major axis of the orbit?

Three bonus questions on astrophysics

a. 40 Eridani B was among the first characterised examples of what type of dense star, which is supported against gravity by electron degeneracy pressure? Sirius B is another example.

b. If a white dwarf gathers enough matter to exceed the Chandrasekhar limit, a mass about 1.4 times that of the Sun, it may undergo runaway thermonuclear fusion resulting in what type of stellar explosion?

c. White dwarfs have a density of approximately a billion kilogrammes per cubic metre. This is far surpassed by what stellar objects, the remnants of other types of supernova?

17 Quote: 'The only genuine consciousness-expanding drug.' These words of Arthur C. Clarke refer to which precise genre of writing?

Three bonus questions on the Solar System

a. In 2011, NASA's Messenger spacecraft sent back images of bright pits or 'hollows', unknown elsewhere in the Solar System and possibly formed by vaporising volatile elements, on the surface of which planet?

b. Before the arrival of Messenger, Mercury had been visited by only one space probe, which first flew by in March 1974. Give both its name and programme number.

c. Mercury's rotation is prograde, with a period exactly two-thirds of its orbital period around the Sun. This means that a day on Mercury lasts how many years?

18 A commercially prosperous state during the seventeenth century, the historical region of Courland is today part of which EU member state?

Three bonus questions on seventeenth-century history

a. After the Restoration, Sir James Scott, the oldest illegitimate son of Charles II, was created the Duke of Buccleuch and which other dukedom?

b. Monmouth led a rebellion against James II that was defeated at which engagement of 1685, the last pitched battle to be fought on English soil?

c. 'The depravity of this man has passed into a proverb.' These words of the historian T.B. Macaulay refer to which judicial figure, involved in the brutal aftermath of the Monmouth rebellion?

19 'Extraversion', 'agreeableness', 'conscientiousness', 'neuroticism' and 'openness to experience or intellect' are considered to be the 'big five' dimensions of what concept in psychology?

Three bonus questions on the psychology of emotion

a. In 1872, which English naturalist published the study entitled *The Expression of the Emotions in Man and Animals*, the first scientific examination of the phenomenon?

b. *The Laws of Emotion* is a work of 2006 by which Dutch psychologist, who claims that emotion is an essentially unconscious process?

c. Born in 1842, and the brother of an eminent novelist, which US psychologist proposed the theory that emotions are caused by physiological responses, rather than vice versa?

20 Lying at the foot of the Chiltern Hills, which estate was bequeathed to the nation in 1921, since when it has been the country residence of the prime minister?

Three bonus questions on religious relics

a. The Church of Santa Croce in Gerusalemme in Rome contains part of a panel reputedly once nailed to Christ's cross and bearing which word, relating to his origins?

b. '... more valuable than precious stones and finer than refined gold'. These words describe the remains of which saint, a second-century bishop of Smyrna who was martyred at the age of 86?

c. Which Indian state is home to the Basilica of Bom Jesus that contains the relics of Saint Francis Xavier?

21 Which mirliton was patented in 1883 by Warren Herbert Frost? A basic type of musical instrument rarely heard in western classical music, it is today most frequently found in the familiar 'submarine' shape.

Three bonus questions on international summits

a. The G7, established in 1976, comprised the G6 of France, the USA, Britain, Germany, Japan and Italy along with which other country?

b. The G8, formed when Russia joined the G7 in 1998, had five countries appended to it in 2005. Mexico and South Africa were two; name two of the other three.

c. In 2009 it was announced that which 'G' group would take over economic discussions from the G8?

22 The name of which country is the origin of the names of a slow dance or promenade, a lively dance in two-four time, and a highly radioactive metallic element discovered by the Curies?

Three bonus questions on adjectives that share the same suffix. In each case, give the word from the definition.

a. An adjective meaning 'holding or grasping firmly', 'stubborn or persistent', or 'tending to stick'?

b. From the Latin for 'to take', an adjective meaning 'capable of holding a lot', 'roomy' or 'spacious'?

c. An adjective that means 'characterised by, or showing, a tendency to talk a great deal'?

23 Which cavities in the human head are blood-filled and called 'venous' when found between the layers of the outer membrane of the brain, and are air-filled and called 'paranasal' in the bones adjoining the nose?

Three bonus questions on the human body

a. What name is given to the point between one nerve cell and another at which the transmission of an impulse takes place?

b. What term denotes a chemical that is released by a nerve-ending on the arrival of an impulse and crosses the synapse to excite or inhibit the post-synaptic cell?

c. The term synapsis is used for the interlocking pairing of homologous chromosomes during what form of cell division, also called reduction division?

24 Listen carefully. If the initial letters of each of the twelve months of the year are written in chronological order, which five-letter boy's name is spelled out as part of the sequence?

Three bonus questions on a month

a. Which month is 'a wicked month', according to the title of a novel of 1965 by the Irish writer Edna O'Brien?

  b. *August 1914* is the first in a series of novels, collectively known as *The Red Wheel*, by which Russian writer?

  c. Which poet wrote that the English winter ended in July, 'to recommence in August'?

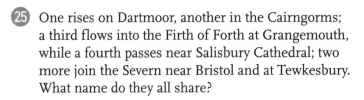 One rises on Dartmoor, another in the Cairngorms; a third flows into the Firth of Forth at Grangemouth, while a fourth passes near Salisbury Cathedral; two more join the Severn near Bristol and at Tewkesbury. What name do they all share?

Three bonus questions on US presidents

  a. As the candidate of the Free Soil Party, which former president won ten per cent of the popular vote at the 1848 presidential election, thus swinging the victory to the Whig, Zachary Taylor?

  b. Who acceded to the presidency on the death of Zachary Taylor in 1850? At the 1856 presidential election he was the candidate of the 'American' or 'Know Nothing' party, and polled twenty-two per cent of the vote.

  c. In the presidential election of 1912, which former president ran as the Progressive Party candidate, attracting twenty-seven per cent of the popular vote?

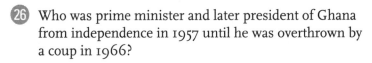 Who was prime minister and later president of Ghana from independence in 1957 until he was overthrown by a coup in 1966?

Three bonus questions on Walt Disney's *Fantasia*

  a. A piece by J.S. Bach opens Disney's *Fantasia* and is an example of what musical form, typically written to show off the technique of the performer? Its name derives from the Latin for 'to touch'.

b. In another scene in *Fantasia*, a troupe of hippopotami wearing tutus dance to the piece 'Dance of the Hours', by which Italian composer?

c. In a scene which apparently lingered in the minds of some of the film's youngest viewers, skeletons rise out of their graves at the behest of a colossal demonic figure to accompany which piece of music?

27 In trigonometry, what term describes the ratio of the length of the hypotenuse to the length of the side opposite an acute angle in a right-angled triangle?

Three bonus questions on non-Euclidean geometry

a. Name the non-Euclidean geometry in which the parallel postulate is replaced by the axiom that any line has at least two parallels through a given point.

b. Name the non-Euclidean geometry in which every line has no parallels through a given point, and in which the sum of the internal angles of every triangle exceeds 180 degrees.

c. 'I have a Euclidean earthly mind, and how could I solve problems that are not of this world?' These words appear in which work of 1880 by Dostoyevsky, his final novel?

28 From a verb meaning to thrash or beat, what adjective is applied to an extra weight carried in horseracing, and also to a boxer or wrestler who is between a light-weight and a middle-weight?

Three bonus questions on biology

a. In which phase of meiosis are bivalent chromosomes attached to the equator of the spindle?

b. Produced by polymerisation of ethanal, what solid is used in horticulture to kill slugs and snails?

c. In vertebrates, what bones articulate with the distal end of metatarsals?

29 'Adulterine' or unauthorised private castles, built by barons, are particularly associated with the reign of which twelfth-century monarch? His civil war with his cousin Matilda is sometimes termed 'the Anarchy'.

Three bonus questions on stamps

a. In 2011, the Royal Mail issued a set of stamps to commemorate the 150th anniversary of the founding of a decorative arts company by which artist, associated with the arts and crafts movement?

b. The mountain gorilla, the African elephant and the red panda are among the animals depicted in another set of stamps issued in 2011, commemorating the 50th anniversary of the founding of which organisation?

c. The 'L & Y.R. 1093 no. 1100' and the 'B.R. W.D. No. 90662' are depicted on a third set of stamps issued in 2011, on what subject?

30 Gateshead Hall, Ferndean Manor, Moor House, Lowood School and Thornfield Hall are among the residences of which eponymous nineteenth-century literary heroine?

Three bonus questions on a polygon

a. A star polygon is denoted by: curly brackets n over m, close brackets; what name is given to the star polygon: curly brackets 5 over 2, close brackets?

b. A pentagram appears on the flags of two African countries. For five points, name both.

c. A pentagram has several examples of the golden ratio, approximately equal to 1.618. Which Greek letter is the symbol for this ratio?

'My abiding memory of my appearance on *University Challenge* is that I got an answer wrong, and in my rage and frustration I let fly with the expletive that begins with "f" for Freddie. It wasn't Ken Tynan who first said it on television, it was me!'

MIRIAM MARGOLYES
(actor)
Contestant, 1962

The Answers

1 *The Picture of Dorian Gray*
- **a.** *The Merry Wives of Windsor* (Falstaff appears in *Henry the Fourth* parts 1 and 2, of course)
- **b.** Herne the Hunter
- **c.** Ralph Vaughan Williams

2 (John) le Carré
- **a.** Eve Arnold
- **b.** Marilyn Monroe
- **c.** Margaret Thatcher

3 Don / Vito Corleone (accept *The Godfather*, correcting it; Marlon Brando and Robert De Niro, of course)
- **a.** Kuwaiti dinar
- **b.** Azerbaijani (new) manat
- **c.** Swiss franc

4 Gordon
- **a.** Fifteenth century
- **b.** Eleventh century
- **c.** Second century

5 *Life and Fate*
- **a.** Belgae (need precise name; pr. Bel-guy or bel-jhee)
- **b.** Bulgars
- **c.** Franks

6 William IV (accept Duke of Clarence, as he was at the time)

    a.   Angela (Carter) and galena
    b.   Adrian and radian (Adrian IV, pope from 1154 to 1159)
    c.   Alfred and flared

7 Steve McQueen
    a.   Wallace Collection
    b.   (Jean Antoine) Watteau (1684–1721; NB Fragonard was later, born 1732, as was Boucher, born 1703)
    c.   Titian

8 Heidelberg
    a.   Aneurism / aneurysm
    b.   Angina pectoris (accept angina)
    c.   Thrombosis

9 Deuteron
    a.   Winston Churchill and L.M. Montgomery
    b.   (Sigmund) Freud and (Robert) Peary
    c.   (Charles) Darwin and (Abraham) Lincoln

10 Fifty (working: $(100 - n)n = 100n - n2$. Differentiating, we see this function has a local maxima/minima at $n = 50$. Since the function is quadratic with negative leading coefficient, this must in fact be a global maxima.)
    a.   Crowdfunding
    b.   Clothes, shoes or other fashion items
    c.   Devo Max

11 $r/2$ (one half r; the resistance is given by rho*l/a where rho=resistivity, l=length and a = cross-sectional area)
    a.   Helium
    b.   (Franz) Hofmeister (1850–1922)
    c.   Minus two

12 Product placement
    a.   Schwa
    b.   Cilia

c. Ascii

13 'This is my truth, tell me yours.'
  a. The Eisteddfod
  b. Avignon Festival / Festival d'Avignon
  c. Hay Festival (of Literature and the Arts)

14 Lausanne
  a. (Joseph E.) Stiglitz
  b. (Nouriel) Roubini
  c. Capitalism

15 Mozilla (the Mozilla Corporation, or MoCo, owned by the Mozilla Foundation)
  a. Folic acid / folate / para-aminobenzoic acid / PABA / vitamin B9 / folacin
  b. Protein synthesis / (ribosomal) translation
  c. Cell walls (accept peptidoglycan or muco-peptide layer of cell walls)

16 3/2 or 1.5
  a. White dwarf (grudgingly accept degenerate dwarf, correcting it)
  b. Type-1(a) supernova (accept supernova, giving the specific type)
  c. Neutron stars

17 Science fiction
  a. Mercury
  b. Mariner 10
  c. Two

18 Latvia
  a. Monmouth (original surname was Crofts but he changed it to Scott)
  b. Sedgemoor

c. Judge Jeffreys (George Jeffreys, 1st Baron Jeffreys of Wem)

19 (Human) personality
- **a.** (Charles) Darwin
- **b.** (Nico) Frijda
- **c.** (William) James (brother of Henry, the novelist; the theory was also independently proposed by Danish scientist Carl Lange)

20 Chequers
- **a.** Nazarene (written in Latin, Greek and Hebrew)
- **b.** Saint Polycarp (in a letter from the church in Smyrna [now Izmir])
- **c.** Goa ('bom' meaning good or holy)

21 Kazoo
- **a.** Canada
- **b.** India / China / Brazil
- **c.** G20

22 Poland (polonaise, polka, polonium)
- **a.** Tenacious
- **b.** Capacious
- **c.** Loquacious

23 Sinuses
- **a.** Synapse
- **b.** Neuro-transmitter
- **c.** Meiosis

24 Jason
- **a.** August (*August Is a Wicked Month*)
- **b.** (Aleksandr) Solzhenitsyn
- **c.** (Lord) Byron (in Don Juan)

25 (River) Avon
- **a.** (Martin) Van Buren
- **b.** (Millard) Fillmore (president 1850–1853)
- **c.** Theodore Roosevelt

26 (Kwame) Nkrumah
- **a.** Toccata (the piece being the Toccata and Fin D Minor)
- **b.** (Amilcare) Ponchielli
- **c.** *Night on the Bare* [or *Bald*] *Mountain* (by Mussorgsky)

27 Cosecant
- **a.** Hyperbolic or Lobachevskian geometry (accept Lobachevski-Bolyai-Gauss geometry or any one of these names)
- **b.** Elliptic / spherical / Riemannian geometry
- **c.** *The Brothers Karazamov*

28 Welter / welterweight (from welt; in horseracing a welterweight is 28 pounds; 40 pounds is a heavy welterweight)
- **a.** First metaphase / metaphase one (if they answer 'metaphase', prompt for more)
- **b.** Metaldehyde (accept meta-aldehyde)
- **c.** Phalanges

29 Stephen (1135–1154)
- **a.** William Morris
- **b.** The WWF / World Wide Fund for Nature / World Wildlife Fund
- **c.** (Classic) locomotives (of England) / (steam) trains

30 Jane Eyre
- **a.** Pentagram (i.e. {n/m} and {5/2} respectively; accept but qualify pentangle or pentalpha; do not accept five-pointed star as we've asked for the name)
- **b.** Morocco and Ethiopia
- **c.** Phi

Match Five

1 Which official EU language is the largest, in terms of speakers, of the West Slavic group?

Three bonus questions on mixtures

a. What term is given to a liquid that boils to give a vapour of an identical composition?

b. Born in 1830, which French scientist gives his name to the equation relating the vapour pressure of an ideal liquid mixture to its composition and the vapour pressures of the pure components?

c. What term denotes a solid solution of two or more components whose freezing point is lower than that of any other possible mixture of these components?

2 A high-level structured programming language developed by Niklaus Wirth; an SI unit equivalent to one newton per square metre, and a 'wager' that argues for belief in the existence of God are all named after which French mathematician and philosopher, born in 1623?

Three bonus questions on cell biology

a. Negri, Cowdry and Guarnieri are among types of inclusion bodies sometimes seen in animal cells. What general type of pathological condition do these bodies indicate?

b. Named after the English doctor who described it in 1817, what degenerative neurological disorder is associated with the appearance in nerve cells of protein aggregates known as Lewy bodies?

c. 'H' inclusions can be demonstrated in cells from patients with alpha thalassemia. In what type of cell do these bodies appear?

3 Listen carefully. The English name of the seat of the Dutch government, the author of *Waiting for Godot*, a leader of the Peasants' Revolt of 1381, and the leader of the opposition from May 2010 link recent holders of which Cabinet office?

Three bonus questions on number theory

a. What adjective describes an integer which is the sum of its distinct positive divisors excluding itself?

b. The only odd prime divisor of an even perfect number takes the form two-to-the-n minus one. After which seventeenth-century French monk are such primes named?

c. What is the smallest perfect number?

4 First performed in 1911 and often given the English title 'Thou Art the Ruler of the Minds of All People', 'Jana Gana Mana' is the national anthem of which country? Its words and music were composed by the Nobel laureate Rabindranath Tagore.

Three bonus questions on nuclear physics

a. Excluding the free neutron, what is the lightest radioactive nuclear isotope, with a half-life of 12.3 years?

b. Tritium contains one proton and two neutrons, each based around three quarks of 'up' and 'down' varieties. In total, how many 'up' quarks and how many 'down' quarks form a tritium nucleus?

c. Tritium decays by emitting a beta particle, resulting in which nuclear isotope with five 'up' and four 'down' quarks? The isotope is present in measurable quantities in lunar soil.

5 Slow worms, like many other lizards, are able to autotomize. This means that, in order to escape predators, they have the ability to do what?

Three bonus questions on a symbol

a. Seen to represent self-reflexivity or the cyclical nature of life, the symbol known by the Greek term *uroboros* takes the form of a serpent or dragon doing what?

b. A self-eating, legless, spherical animal may have been the first living thing in the universe, according to Timaeus in the dialogue by which Greek philosopher?

c. The German chemist August Kekulé sometimes claimed that a daydream of a snake seizing its own tail inspired him in his discovery of the structure of which molecule?

6 Who is depicted in a statue unveiled in December 2010, on the base of which are inscribed the words: 'That Whitsun I was late getting away'?

Three bonus questions on zoology. I want the common English name of the following British mammals.

a. *Talpa europaea*, a small, carnivorous mammal?

b. *Meles meles*, a large, distinctively patterned omnivore?

c. *Phoca vitulina*, a sleek, aquatic piscivore?

7 Believed to be the largest reliquary in the western world, the Shrine of the Three Kings, traditionally thought to contain the remains of the biblical Magi, is located above the high altar of which cathedral in Germany?

Three bonus questions on US place names

a. Founded by William Penn, which major city shares its name with that of a community in Asia Minor, the sixth of the Seven Churches, according to the Book of Revelation, to receive letters containing messages from God?

b. Its name derived from the place in Ephraim where, according to some sources, the Ark of the Covenant was once kept, which church meeting-house in Tennessee gives its name to a battle of 1862 also known as the Battle of Pittsburg (sic) Landing?

c. Which city is the largest in Tennessee and takes its name from that of an ancient capital, also known as Noph, mentioned by Isaiah, Jeremiah and other prophets in their condemnation of Israel's misplaced trust in Egypt?

8 In physics, Bragg's law applies to the scattering of X-rays from what?

Three bonus questions on shorter words that can be made using any of the nine letters of the word 'epeolatry', meaning, of course, 'the worship of words'. In each case, give the word from the definition.

a. The national gemstone of Australia, a form of hydrated silica, noted for rich iridescence and the play of changing colours?

b. A game of Basque origin, in which players hurl a ball against a marked wall using a basket-like racket strapped to the wrist?

c. Mechanical or habitual repetition of something to be learned, often without regard to meaning; for example, as in preparation for a quiz?

9 'Half of the American people have never read a newspaper. Half have never voted for a president. One hopes it is the same half.' These are the words of which satirist and political writer, the author of several novels including *The City and the Pillar* and *The Golden Age*, who died in August 2012?

Three bonus questions on wit

a. 'True wit is nature to advantage dressed, / What oft was thought, but ne'er so well expressed.' Which poet wrote these words in the 1711 work *Essay on Criticism*?

b. 'The man I thought had been a lord among wits; but, I find, he is only a wit among lords.' Which literary figure said this of Lord Chesterfield in 1754?

c. 'Brevity is the soul of wit.' In which play by Shakespeare do these words appear?

10 What five-letter term, the Greek for 'branch', was coined by the biologist Julian Huxley in the 1950s for a group of organisms that have evolved from a common ancestor, such as the class Aves, the birds?

Three questions on a term from the Greek

a. From the Greek meaning 'a stoppage', what noun means a slowing or halting of the normal flow of body fluids, or a state of equilibrium?

b. In ancient Greek history, for example the works of Thucydides, the term 'stasis' denotes what political situation?

c. 'Stasis in darkness. / Then the substanceless blue / Pour of tor and distances.' These words begin the poem 'Ariel' by which US-born writer?

11. 'A liquor made of apples, sugar and ale; a drunken bout; a merry song.' These were Doctor Johnson's definitions in 1755 of which seven-letter word associated with the Christmas season?

Three bonus questions on proper names in which no letter is repeated, sometimes called 'isograms'. In each case, give the name from the description.

a. A town in north Lincolnshire, noted for steel production?

b. An automotive company founded by the German government in 1937?

c. The eleven-letter English name of a landlocked European country?

12. Which fictional character had, among his campaign medals, the Egypt Medal, the Queen's Sudan Medal, and the 1914 Star? The actor playing him died in November 2012.

Three bonus questions on French towns and cities that lie close to the Prime, or Greenwich, Meridian. In each case, name the place from the description.

a. The capital of the historical province of Maine; its motor-racing circuit is home to a well-known endurance race.

b. The capital of the Calvados department, 15 kilometres from the English Channel; much of it was destroyed following the Normandy invasion in 1944.

c. A pilgrimage centre in the foothills of the Pyrenees; it was the birthplace, in 1844, of the religious figure Bernadette Soubirous.

13 Indicating the monies that cooks collected from the sale of leftover fat, grease and watery food, what two-word term deriving from nautical slang has come to denote a reserve of money used for illicit purposes such as political bribery?

Three bonus questions on a car manufacturer

a. One of the biggest flops in motor industry history, the 1958 Edsel car was named after the son of which manufacturer?

b. Born in 1891, which Sardinian Marxist coined the term 'Fordism' to illustrate how new American production techniques signalled the start of a new epoch in capitalist development?

c. The Forgotten Jungle City of Fordlandia was Ford's attempt to recreate small-town America, and secure cheap rubber, in the rainforest of which country?

14 In his 1993 paper 'The Deadweight Loss of Christmas', the US economist Joel Waldfogel investigated the losses of value that result from which holiday tradition?

Three bonus questions on royal appointments. In each case, give the position that all three of the following have held.

a. Nicholas Staggins, Walford Davies and Arthur Bliss?

b. Benjamin West, Anthony Blunt and Desmond Shawe-Taylor?

c. Nathaniel Bliss, Richard van der Riet Woolley and Arnold Wolfendale?

15 Quote: '[People] are buying the books because the books invite them to be submissive too, not to punishment, but to a 1980s-style dominance of money and power and products. The word "flog" has more than one meaning.' These words in the *London Review of Books* refer to which recent trilogy?

Three bonus questions on psychiatry and psychoanalysis

a. *The Sane Society* and *The Art of Loving* are among works by which US psychoanalyst, born in Germany in 1900?

b. Which Frankfurt-born psychologist's theory of psychosocial development advanced his belief that personality develops in a series of stages? He published *Childhood and Society* in 1950.

c. Which Canadian-born psychiatrist introduced Transactional Analysis in his 1964 work *Games People Play*?

16 An Olympic event since 2000, the name of which martial art means 'the way of hand and foot' in Korean?

Three bonus questions on information dispersal

a. Now used almost entirely in a derogatory sense, what word for the spreading of information comes from the name of a committee of cardinals founded in 1622 by Pope Gregory XV?

b. Who pioneered the field of public relations and the manipulation of public opinion, calling it the 'engineering of consent'? A nephew of Sigmund Freud, he was the author in 1928 of the work *Propaganda*.

c. Which 2002 television documentary series by Adam Curtis explained how Bernays repackaged Freud's ideas for the purposes of public relations in the USA?

17 Around 440 kilometres in length, the Loa is the longest river of which South American country? Rising near the Bolivian border, it flows southwest from the mountains and then across the Atacama desert, before emptying into the Pacific.

Three bonus questions on university scholarships

a. Which crime writer has launched a series of scholarships for Sheffield University students in the name of his military policeman character Jack Reacher?

b. Benjamin Franklin chemistry scholarships are awarded by which Scottish university? In 1759, it awarded Franklin an honorary doctorate in law, and in 2002 unveiled a permanent tribute to him.

c. What is the world's oldest international scholarship programme, allowing exceptional postgraduate students from various countries to study at Oxford University?

18 Answer as soon as your name is called. In ternary, or base three, a one followed by three zeroes represents what number in decimal?

Three bonus questions on mathematics

a. The quadratic equation $ax^2 + bx + c = 0$ has a repeated, or double, root if the quantity $b^2 - 4ac = 0$. What name is given to this quantity?

b. What is the numerical value of the repeated, or double, root of the equation: $4x^2 + 4x + 1$?

c. The equation $(x^3 + 4x^2 + 5x + 2 = 0)$ has a double root at $x = -1$. What is the value of its other root?

19 'Everything considered, a determined soul will always manage.' Which French thinker made this statement in the 1942 work *The Myth of Sisyphus*?

Three bonus questions on New York

a. Associated with amusement parks and the birth of the hot dog, which peninsula lies in the southernmost part of the New York borough of Brooklyn?

b. In 1609, which British explorer, commanding the *Half-Moon*, put in at Coney Island before continuing into what is now New York Harbor?

c. Which film by Woody Allen includes a sequence in which his character's childhood home is revealed to be at the foot of a Coney Island rollercoaster?

20 Formerly used to produce acetylene in lamps, which solid grey compound has the chemical formula CaC_2?

Three bonus questions on organic chemistry

a. In chemistry, the symbol 'R' is used for which group, formed from an alkane by the removal of a single hydrogen atom?

b. What name is given to the simplest alkyl group, also known as the CH_3 group?

c. Which of the methyls is a flammable toxic liquid, used as a solvent and anti-freeze? It can be catalytically converted to petrol, and has the formula CH_3OH?

21 'Am toast' is an anagram of what botanical term, indicating the openings in a leaf through which transpiration takes place?

Three bonus questions on bays

a. The Great Australian Bight, lying between Cape Pasley, Western Australia and Cape Carnot, South Australia, is a bay of which ocean?

b. The shipping area German Bight was formerly named after which bay at the mouth of the Elbe river, the site of naval battles in 1914 and 1917, and an aerial battle in 1939?

c. The Bight of Bonny was formerly named after which secessionist West African state that declared its independence from Nigeria in 1967?

22 What letter and number designated the model of Lockheed high-altitude reconnaissance aircraft, one of which was piloted by Gary Powers and shot down over the Soviet Union in 1960?

Three bonus questions on a statesman

a. Then a relatively unknown army officer, which future head of state made 'the appeal of June the 18th' to his countrymen on BBC Radio in 1940?

b. 'If the Germans are beaten, General de Gaulle will return. He will be supported ... by 80 or 90 per cent of the French people, and I shall be hanged.' Which French politician made this prescient remark in late 1943? He was executed in 1945.

c. 'He left France smaller than he found it, true; but you can't measure a nation like that. As far as France is concerned, he had to happen.' This observation of Charles de Gaulle refers to which historical figure?

23 What six-letter word may indicate both a former British army rank, the equivalent of the modern second lieutenant, and a flag or standard used by military or naval units?

Three bonus questions on first laws

a. Newton's first law of motion, stating that an object that is in motion will not change its velocity unless a force acts upon it, is also known as the law of what?

b. 'Everything is related to everything else, but near things are more related to each other.' This statement by the American-Swiss academic Waldo Tobler has been described as the 'first law' of which academic subject?

c. 'To seek peace, and follow it', but 'by all means we can, to defend ourselves' is the first or fundamental law of nature according to which English philosopher in his 1651 work *Leviathan*?

24 Completed in 1910, *Treemonisha* is an opera by which African-American composer, better known for piano compositions such as 'Pineapple Rag' and 'The Maple Leaf Rag'?

Three bonus questions on the Civil Rights Movement

a. Formed in 1964, the organisation known as the OAAU was a major campaigning group on civil rights issues in the 1960s. For what do the letters AAU stand?

b. Which civil rights campaigner formed the OAAU and was assassinated a year later?

c. Who was the president of the USA when the 1964 Civil Rights Act was passed?

25 Who became chancellor of the Exchequer in 1533? An instigator of the dissolution of the monasteries, he was executed in 1540.

Three bonus questions on chancellors of the Exchequer

a. Which chancellor introduced the 'People's Budget', whose rejection by the Lords led to the Parliament Act of 1910?

b. Which Labour chancellor nationalised the Bank of England in 1946 then resigned his office in November of the following year, having leaked details of the autumn Budget to a journalist?

c. Which chancellor's 'broken cricket bats' resignation speech of 1990 is widely considered to have precipitated the downfall of Margaret Thatcher three weeks later?

26 *The Derby at Epsom* and *Portrait of a Kleptomaniac* are among the works of which French artist, born in 1791? He is perhaps best known for a startling painting of a shipwreck, known as *The Raft of the Medusa*.

Three bonus questions on artists born in the 1880s

a. Active mainly in Paris, which Italian artist is noted for portraiture characterised by asymmetrical compositions and elongated figures? His dissolute lifestyle contributed to an early death from tuberculosis.

b. Noted for his depictions of Montmartre, which French artist received the name by which he is known from a Spanish art critic, who recognised him as his son in order to help him?

c. Which Russian-born artist and designer is noted for his illustrations of La Fontaine's Fables and for stained glass such as that in Tudeley church in Kent? He gives his name to a museum in Nice.

27 A meditation on the nature of love, which of the Romantic poets was the author in 1821 of the poem *Epipsychidion*?

Three bonus questions on a poet

a. When in 1601 his secret marriage to Ann More became known, which poet and clergyman was briefly imprisoned and dismissed from his role as Secretary to the Lord Keeper of the Great Seal?

b. Which insect is the title of a poem by Donne in which the speaker tries to convince his lover that by crushing the insect she commits 'three sinnes in killing three'?

c. Which five words from a meditation by Donne did Ernest Hemingway take as the title of a 1940 novel, set in Spain?

28 Behemoth, cherub, jubilee and leviathan are among English words that derive ultimately from which language of West Asia?

Three bonus questions on sleep

a. For what do the letters REM stand in the stage of the human sleeping cycle characterised by vivid dreaming?

b. After a Greek letter, what name denotes the low-frequency, high-amplitude waves that appear increasingly in the dreamless advanced stages of non-REM sleep?

c. Into how many stages is the non-REM sleep phase usually subdivided, each indicating a deeper sleep than the previous one?

29 John W. Young in 1981 and Chris Ferguson in 2011 were the first and last commanders of which series of NASA missions?

Three bonus questions on cosmology

a. The 2011 Nobel prize in Physics was awarded for the discovery that the expansion of the universe is accelerating, a phenomenon also known as dark energy. Give me the surname of any one of the three recipients.

b. In 2013, NASA joined the European Space Agency's mission to investigate the nature of dark energy. Which ancient author, whose works include *The Elements*, gives his name to this mission?

c. The Euclid mission may reveal whether the density of dark energy is variable, as it would be according to a theory named after the classical 'fifth element', known by what name?

30 Which comedy by Shakespeare is the source of the opera by Berlioz entitled *Béatrice and Bénédict*?

Three bonus questions on a play by Shakespeare

a. Milton's *Comus* and Auden's collection *The Sea and the Mirror* are among the works inspired by which of Shakespeare's later plays?

b. Its characters including Robby the Robot and Doctor Edward Morbius, which 1956 science fiction film is noted for its many similarities to *The Tempest*?

c. Described as a 'Fantasia after Shakespeare's Drama', *The Tempest* is an 1873 work by which Russian composer?

The Answers

1 Polish (Czech and Slovak are the other two main West Slavic languages)
   a. Azeotrope / azeotropic / azeotropic mixture
   b. (François-Marie) Raoult (1830–1901; Raoult's law)
   c. Eutectic / eutectic mixture

2 (Blaise) Pascal
   a. Virus / viral infection (respectively, rabies; herpes simplex, varicella-zoster, cytomegalovirus; smallpox)
   b. Parkinson's disease (James Parkinson, 1755–1824; also in Lewy body dementia and Alzheimer's but neither of these answer the first clause: Frederic Lewy, born Berlin 1885; Alois Alzheimer, born Bavaria 1864)
   c. Erythrocytes / red blood cells

3 Foreign secretary (Hague, Beckett, Straw, Miliband)
   a. Perfect
   b. (Marin) Mersenne
   c. 6 (working: the only divisor of 1 is 1 itself; 2, 3 and 5 are all prime, so cannot be perfect; the divisors of 4 are 1, 2 and 4, and 1 + 2 = 3. 6 is certainly perfect since its proper divisors are 1, 2 and 3)

4 India
   a. Tritium (also known as hydrogen-3)
   b. Four 'up' and five 'down'
   c. Helium-3

5 Shed their tails (the tail regrows but remains smaller)
- **a.** Devouring its own tail (and being reborn)
- **b.** Plato
- **c.** Benzene (ring)

6 Philip Larkin (in Hull, marking the 25th anniversary of his death)
- **a.** (European, northern, common) mole
- **b.** (European) badger
- **c.** Common / harbour seal (accept 'seal', adding type)

7 Cologne / Köln
- **a.** Philadelphia
- **b.** Shiloh (Pittsburg Landing was a steamboat docking point in the area)
- **c.** Memphis

8 A crystal lattice (accept crystal)
- **a.** Opal
- **b.** Pelota
- **c.** Rote

9 Gore Vidal
- **a.** (Alexander) Pope
- **b.** (Doctor Samuel) Johnson
- **c.** *Hamlet*

10 Clade
- **a.** Stasis
- **b.** Party factional feuds / civil strife / internal disturbances (accept similar)
- **c.** Sylvia Plath

11 Wassail
- **a.** Scunthorpe
- **b.** Volkswagen
- **c.** Switzerland

12 Lance-Corporal (Jack) Jones (Clive Dunn in *Dad's Army*, of course)
- **a.** Le Mans
- **b.** Caen
- **c.** Lourdes

13 Slush fund
- **a.** Henry Ford
- **b.** (Antonio) Gramsci
- **c.** Brazil

14 Gift-giving / giving presents/ exchanging gifts ('an orgy of wealth destruction', in his words)
- **a.** Master of the Queen's / King's Music (1674–1700, 1934–1941, 1942–1953)
- **b.** Surveyor of the Queen's / King's Pictures (1791–1820, 1945–1972, 2005–; not Surveyor of the Queen's Works of Art, which is a separate post although sometimes held by the same person as the above title)
- **c.** Astronomer Royal (1762–1764, 1956–1971, 1991–1995)

15 *Fifty Shades* (by E.L. James; accept *Fifty Shades of Grey*)
- **a.** (Erich) Fromm
- **b.** (Erik) Erikson
- **c.** (Eric) Berne

16 Tae Kwon Do
- **a.** Propaganda (Congregatio de Propaganda Fide)
- **b.** (Edward) Bernays
- **c.** *The Century of the Self*

17 Chile
- **a.** Lee Child (b. Jim Grant; Child is a visiting professor and graduate of the university)
- **b.** St Andrews
- **c.** Rhodes Scholarships

18 27 (i.e. $3^3 = 1$, $3^2 = 0$, $3 = 0$, units $= 0$)
  a. Discriminant
  b. -½ (minus one-half)
  c. -2 (minus two)

19 (Albert) Camus
  a. Coney Island
  b. (Henry) Hudson
  c. *Annie Hall*

20 Calcium carbide
  a. Alkyl (group)
  b. Methyl (group)
  c. Methanol / methyl alcohol / wood alcohol

21 Stomata
  a. Indian
  b. Heligoland (Bight)
  c. Biafra (Bight of Biafra)

22 U2 (nicknamed Dragon Lady)
  a. (Charles) de Gaulle
  b. (Pierre) Laval (not Petain, who was also sentenced to death but the sentence was not carried out because of his age; he died in 1951. Laval was twice head of the Vichy government.)
  c. Napoleon (the First)

23 Ensign
  a. Inertia
  b. Geography
  c. (Thomas) Hobbes

24 Scott Joplin
  a. Afro-American Unity (accept 'African-American Unity', correcting it)

b.   Malcolm X / Malcolm Little
c.   Lyndon B. Johnson

25 Thomas Cromwell
    a.   (David) Lloyd George
    b.   (Hugh) Dalton
    c.   (Sir Geoffrey) Howe

26 (Théodore) Géricault
    a.   (Amedeo) Modigliani (1884–1920)
    b.   (Maurice) Utrillo (1883–1955)
    c.   (Marc) Chagall (1887–1985)

27 (Percy Bysshe) Shelley
    a.   John Donne
    b.   'The Flea'
    c.   'For whom the bell tolls'

28 Hebrew
    a.   Rapid Eye Movement
    b.   Delta (waves)
    c.   Four

29 Space Shuttle or Space Transportation System (STS) flights
    a.   (Saul) Perlmutter / (Brain) Schmidt / (Adam) Riess
    b.   Euclid
    c.   Quintessence

30 *Much Ado about Nothing*
    a.   *The Tempest*
    b.   *Forbidden Planet*
    c.   Tchaikovsky

Match Six

1 In astrophysics, the abbreviation AGN stands for what three-word classification, sub-classes of which include Quasars, Blazars and Seyferts?

Three bonus questions on radiation

a. What term is used to describe electromagnetic radiation with wavelengths in the approximate range of 0.01 to 10 nanometres, and energy between 0.12 and 120 kilo electron volts?

b. The first cosmic X-ray astronomy satellite, launched from the San Marco platform off the coast of Kenya in 1970, was given what name, the Swahili for 'freedom'?

c. The strongest known extra-solar source of X-rays, the double star Scorpius X-1, around 9,000 light years away, is what type of stellar remnant?

2 In 1997, who became the world's first woman to be elected to succeed another woman as head of state? The female in question easily won a second term in 2004 as she was the only validly nominated candidate.

Three bonus questions on counties of the Republic of Ireland

a. In an alphabetical list of the twenty-six counties of the Republic of Ireland, which comes first?

b. Three counties in the Republic of Ireland have a name beginning with 'M'. Name two of them.

    c. Only one county in the Republic of Ireland has a name beginning with the letter 'S'. What is it?

3 By weight percentage, what is the third largest elemental constituent of seawater, after oxygen and hydrogen?

Three bonus questions on atomic structure

    a. In atoms, electron shells are sub-divided into sub-shells. The lowest energy sub-shell is given the symbol lower-case 's'. What lower-case symbol denotes the next lowest?

    b. How many unpaired electrons are there in the ground state of an atom of oxygen, given that the atomic number of oxygen is 8?

    c. Chlorine has an atomic number of 17. How many 3p electrons are there in a chlorine atom?

4 *Cape Fear*, *The Age of Innocence* and *The Last Temptation of Christ* are among the works of which film director, born in New York in 1942?

Three bonus questions on the Solar System. In each case, name the planet whose minor moons include the following.

    a. Themisto, Adrastea, Pasiphaë, Leda and Himalia?

    b. Sycorax, Prospero, Margaret, Perdita and Mab?

    c. Skoll, Fenrir, Atlas, Pandora and Pan?

5 In mathematics, what four-letter word denotes the hyperbolic function given by the formula e-to-the-z plus e-to-the-minus-z all divided by two?

Three bonus questions on an Islamic mathematician

a. The ninth-century Islamic mathematician al-Kwarizmi wrote an influential treatise on numeration that gave us which word for a recursive, terminating mathematical procedure?

b. Which notational system developed in India did al-Kwarizmi popularise in the same book?

c. Another treatise of al-Kwarizmi, entitled *The Compendious Book on Calculation by Completion and Balancing*, gave rise to the name of which branch of modern mathematics?

6 The official residence of the holder of which political office is Bute House, located at 6 Charlotte Square in Edinburgh?

Three bonus questions on anthems

a. Which unofficial national anthem was composed in the 1960s by Roy Williamson, a member of folk group The Corries?

b. Standardised in the 1990s, which country's national anthem includes verses sung in five different languages?

c. In 2001, which country readopted, with different words, an anthem that had been in use from 1944 until 1991?

7 Listen carefully and answer as soon as your name is called. In joules, what is the kinetic energy of a ball with mass 2 kilograms travelling with momentum 10 kilogram metres per second?

Three bonus questions on Chinese literature

a. Sima Qian is often described as the 'father of Chinese historiography' and wrote a history of China from the Yellow Emperor until his own time. During which dynasty did he live?

b. The poets Wang Wei, Du Fu and Li Bai (also known as Li Po) all lived during which dynasty?

c. Which dynasty saw the publication of the vernacular fiction works *Journey to the West*, also known as *Monkey*, and *The Plum in the Golden Vase*, sometimes described as the *Fanny Hill* of Chinese literature?

8 To the nearest whole degree, how many degrees are there in one radian?

Three bonus questions on twentieth-century French theatre

a. The works of which French playwright include *Antigone* in 1943 and *Becket* in 1959, the latter being adapted for the cinema with Richard Burton in the title role?

b. One of the most prominent French playwrights of the late twentieth century, whose work includes *Sallinger*, *Roberto Zucco* and *In the Solitude of the Cotton Fields*?

c. Which 1995 play by Yasmina Reza concerns the argument between three friends over a 200,000-franc white-on-white painting?

9 'Wars begin when you will, but they do not end when you please.' This statement appears in *The History of Florence*, a 1524 work by which political philosopher?

Three bonus questions on international relations

a. From the Latin for 'to command', which term refers to the relationship of a hegemonic state to subordinate states, nations or peoples under its control?

b. In his 1902 critique *Imperialism*, which English economist linked the phenomenon with the demands of maturing capitalism for raw materials and cheap labour?

c. Which revolutionary figure revived Hobson's thesis in the 1916 pamphlet *Imperialism: The Highest Stage of Capitalism*?

10 Give the single word that completes this observation of Napoleon I: 'There is only one step from the sublime to the...' what?

Three bonus questions on political figures born in 1770. In each case, name the person from the description.

a. In office from 1812 to 1827, a prime minister remembered for the years of political and social repression after the Napoleonic Wars?

b. A former leader of the House of Commons, he was killed by Stephenson's *Rocket* at the opening of the Liverpool to Manchester Railway in 1830?

c. Briefly prime minister in 1827, as foreign secretary he had supported the Greek revolt against the Turks, and the independence of Spain's Latin American colonies?

11 20 Maresfield Gardens in Hampstead and Berggasse 19 in the Alsergrund district of Vienna are now both museums, having been the homes of which psychoanalyst, who died in London in 1939?

Three bonus questions on historic buildings, in the words of the author Simon Jenkins

a. 'Completed in 1588 for Sir Francis Willoughby, a fussy, learned and increasingly demented tycoon who had made his fortune from (local) coal.' These words describe Wollaton Hall, in which English city?

b. 'The hall's interior is sensational ... the uprights are beautifully moulded and the quatrefoils on the walls have an almost jazzy effect.' These words refer to the fifteenth-century Ordsall Hall, in which city?

c. 'A place of which [its city] can be proud ... It ranks among the great Jacobean houses of the north.' These words describe Temple Newsam, in which English city?

12 The Penrose triangle is an impossible figure that inspired *Ascending and Descending*, a 1960 work by which Dutch artist who is known for realistic, detailed lithographs that achieve optical and conceptual effects?

Three bonus questions on websites

a. Founded by the former Facebook employees Charlie Cheever and Adam d'Angelo, which question-and-answer site provides content from experts including Steve Case and Jimmy Wales, the co-founders of AOL and Wikipedia respectively?

b. Ben Silbermann was a co-founder in 2010 of which 'virtual pinboard', which allows users to organise and share images, events and interests?

c. Using the slogan 'Follow the world's creators', which blog-hosting platform was founded in 2007 by David Karp to post and customise text, images, links and content from a desktop or phone?

13 Which year of the twentieth century saw the deaths of Samuel Beckett, Daphne du Maurier and Salvador Dalí, along with major unrest in China and a wave of revolutions in Eastern Europe?

Three bonus questions on twentieth-century politicians

a. Who was the first UK prime minister to have been born in the twentieth century? He is also the only one to have played first-class cricket.

b. Who was the first French president to have been born in the twentieth century?

c. Who was the first US president to have been born in the twentieth century?

14 Also denoting small, cat-like mammals found in Asia and Africa, what six-letter acronym is used in financial circles for a group of emerging markets including Columbia, Vietnam and South Africa?

Three bonus questions on US state mottos, specifically, those in languages other than English and Latin

a. What is the only US state to have an Italian motto? Often translated as 'Strong deeds, gentle words', it was the motto of the English peer Cecilius Calvert, who named the original colony after the Catholic queen of Charles I.

b. The northernmost US state after Alaska, which state has the French *L'Etoile du Nord*, or 'Star of the North', as its motto?

c. Montana is the only state with a Spanish motto, *Oro y plata*, referring to which two metals?

15 Which city in the French Basque country is noted for the production of both a sweet liqueur called Izarra and an air-dried salted ham, and is believed to have given its name to an edged weapon usually fixed to the muzzle of a musket or rifle?

Three bonus questions on sausages

a. What name for a type of small sausage comes from the Italian word for 'onion', and was originally applied to an onion stew?

b. Which city of south-western France gives its name to a sausage of coarse-ground pork, often used in cassoulet?

c. In 2011, which coiled English sausage was successful in its bid for 'protected geographical indication' status under EU law?

16 What polygon links: the eighteen segments of the James Webb Space Telescope mirror; twenty of the faces of the Buckminsterfullerene molecule; most of the basalt columns in the Giant's Causeway; and the wax cells of a honeycomb?

Three bonus questions on censorship

a. Quote: 'Without incurring the danger of being hurt with any indelicacy of expression, [the reader] may learn in the fate of Macbeth, that even a kingdom is dearly purchased, if virtue be the price of acquisition.' These are the words of which editor, referring to his nineteenth-century editions of Shakespeare?

b. Bowdler's *Family Shakespeare* omits entirely the character of Doll Tearsheet, a prostitute, from which of Shakespeare's histories?

c. Published posthumously in 1826 under the supervision of his nephew, Bowdler's last work was an expurgated version of which six-volume history, published from 1776?

17 In words such as 'chrysanthemum' and 'chrysalis', the Greek prefix 'chrys' refers to which metal?

Three bonus questions on British currency

a. In 1696, which architect, a founder of the Royal Society, proposed a decimal coinage based on a silver noble divided into ten primes and one hundred seconds?

b. Equivalent to one-tenth of a pound and named ultimately after an Italian city, which coin was introduced in 1849 as a tentative step towards a decimal currency?

c. In which decade was full decimalisation finally introduced in the United Kingdom?

18 South Sudan became the world's newest nation in July 2011 with an independence ceremony in which city, serving as its capital?

Three bonus questions on glands

a. What collective name is given to those glands in the human body that secrete hormones directly into the bloodstream?

b. Located below the larynx, which endocrine gland secretes hormones vital to metabolism and growth?

c. The adrenal glands are small endocrine glands located immediately above which organs of the body?

19 Having a 500-year history, which building has been a poor house, a mental institution and, in the seventeenth century, the hunting lodge of the Elector of Saxony? More recently part of it was transformed into a youth hostel to encourage people to escape to it, rather than from it.

Three bonus questions on prisons

a. Dartmoor Prison was originally built to house what general category of prisoner?

b. Used to house paramilitary prisoners, which prison in County Antrim was also known as Long Kesh? It closed in 2000.

c. Situated on the outskirts of Glasgow, which is Scotland's largest and most complex penal establishment?

20 Proust's *A la recherche du temps perdu* and other series of novels linked by common characters or preoccupations are sometimes referred to by what two-word French term, literally meaning 'river novel'?

Three bonus questions on the verb 'to be' in the Romance languages

a. The third-person singular imperfect of the verb 'to be' in both Catalan and Italian spells the name of which subdivision of geological time in English?

b. The third-person plural present tense of the verb *ser* in Spanish spells what common English word?

c. The third-person singular present of the verb 'to be' in French spells which compass direction in the same language?

21 During the seventeenth century, the main plot and the by-plot were both directed against which king? The first aimed to replace him with his cousin Arabella Stuart, and the second to kidnap him and compel him to grant toleration to Roman Catholics.

Three bonus questions on names

a. Which explorer gives his name to the strait that lies between the south of mainland South America and the north of Tierra del Fuego?

b. Which explorer gives his name to the strait that lies between Cape Dezhnev in Russia and Cape Prince of Wales in Alaska?

c. Which explorer gives his name to the strait that lies between the north island and south island of New Zealand?

22 In 2011, which story for children was adapted by the Royal Ballet to become the first new, full-length ballet made for the company for fifteen years?

Three bonus questions on lost hands

a. Which major literary figure lost the use of his left hand as a result of wounds sustained during the Battle of Lepanto in 1571?

b. Lord Nelson's right hand and arm were amputated as a result of wounds received during a landing in 1797 at which of the Canary Islands?

c. Later a commander in the Crimean War, which soldier had his right hand amputated after Waterloo, and gave his name to a type of sleeve that was designed for him to wear after his injuries?

23 Which city to the south-east of Amsterdam gives its name to a 'school' of Dutch painters, including Van Honthorst and Terbrugghen, who went to Rome in the early seventeenth century and were influenced by the works of Caravaggio?

Three bonus questions on biology

a. What name is given to the ribonucleoprotein on which protein synthesis takes place in living cells?

b. What term denotes the process by which an RNA polymerase enzyme creates a new RNA molecule using an existing DNA strand as a template?

c. Which pyrimidine base of an RNA strand is paired with the adenine base of a DNA strand when RNA and DNA strands are aligned during transcription?

24 Answer as soon as your name is called. Which girl's name can be spelled out using the letters of the NATO spelling alphabet that denote a Spanish word for a mountain range, a populous country of South Asia, a Greek letter, and a month?

Three bonus questions on words. In each case, give the term from the definition. All three have the same four final letters.

a. A debilitating viral disease transmitted by mosquitos; it causes sudden fever and acute pain in the joints, hence its alternative name of 'breakbone fever'?

b. In linguistics, language seen as an abstract system used by a speech community, as distinct from the instances of its use by individuals?

c. Finally, a lengthy, aggressive speech, tirade or lecture?

25 What rank in the modern British army links a period of direct military government during Oliver Cromwell's protectorate with a patter song in Gilbert and Sullivan's *The Pirates of Penzance*?

Three bonus questions on Restoration drama

a. ''Tis better to be left than never to have been loved.' Thought to have inspired a similar line by Tennyson, these words are spoken by Mrs Marwood in *The Way of the World* by which dramatist?

b. Sir Fopling Flutter is the title character in which comedy, first performed in 1676 and written by Sir George Etherege?

c. *The Provok'd Wife* is a Restoration comedy by which playwright, also known as the architect of Castle Howard and Blenheim Palace?

26 'His music suffers from lack of emotional range, often deteriorating into fairy-like Prestos and sugary sentimental Andantes. His violin concerto characterises this criticism, yet its charm almost defies it.' These words, from *Chambers Biographical Dictionary*, refer to which German composer, born in 1809, whose works include the 'Italian' symphony and the *Hebrides Overture*?

Three bonus questions on zoology

a. Calamus, rachis and barbules are features on which specialised epidermal structures of some vertebrates?

b. To which bone of a bird's wing are secondary flight feathers attached?

c. In avian anatomy, which large muscles are attached to the humerus and are responsible for the down-stroke of the wings, thus supporting the bird in flight?

27 What part of speech or lexical category links a horror novel of 1986 by Stephen King, a dystopian novel of 1921 by Yevgeny Zamyatin, and an adventure novel of 1886 by Henry Rider Haggard?

Three bonus questions on novels with the same number in their titles

a. Set in Japan in 1799, which novel by David Mitchell relates the story of a young Dutch clerk who hopes to make his fortune there?

b. Based on Shakespeare's *King Lear*, which Pulitzer Prize-winning novel by Jane Smiley is set in Iowa in the late twentieth century?

c. Which novel by Khaled Hosseini follows the lives of two Afghan women, Laila and Mariam, in a story which covers the history of Afghanistan from the 1960s to the early twenty-first century?

28 In his year-end press conference of December 2004, the then UN Secretary-General, Kofi Annan, used what two-word phrase to describe that particularly difficult year? It is more commonly associated with a speech by the Queen at the London Guildhall in November 1992.

Three bonus questions on clouds. In each case, identify the cloud type from the two-letter abbreviation used by the World Meteorological Organisation:

a. Cu?

b. Cc?

c. Ac?

29 At Gresham College in London in the seventeenth century, an intellectual circle organised itself 'for the promoting of physico-mathematical experimental learning'. After obtaining the patronage of the restored monarch, this group became known by what name?

Three bonus questions on presidents of the Royal Society

a. The president of the Royal Society from 1727 to 1741, Sir Hans Sloane's estate formed part of the original collection of which national institution?

b. Joseph Banks was the president of the Royal Society for more than forty years; from 1768 to 1771, he had served as naturalist on which navigator's voyage of discovery?

c. Joseph Hooker became the president of the Royal Society in 1873, and also served for twenty years as the director of which institution in south-west London?

30 What two-word term denotes the small interval that is the difference between twelve just perfect fifths and seven octaves, corresponding to the frequency ratio three to the power of twelve over two to the power of nineteen?

Three bonus questions on opera. Name the operas that match the following descriptions, and give the composer in each case.

a. A work first performed in 1816, in which Count Almaviva pursues Rosina?

b. Nemorino attempts to win Adina, a wealthy farm owner, by means of the substance in the opera's title; it was first performed in Milan in 1832?

c. An opera first performed in Vienna in 1791, in which the lovers Tamino and Pamina must endure trials in order to be united?

'You have to get the trick of pressing the buzzer when you think you might know the answer.'

JULIAN FELLOWES
(actor and Oscar-winning screenwriter)
Contestant, 1969

The Answers

1 Active Galactic Nucleus
- **a.** X-rays or X radiation
- **b.** Uhuru
- **c.** Neutron star (i.e. the gravitational collapse of a massive star during a Type II, Type Ib or Type Ic supernova event; not supernova remnant, which is something else)

2 Mary McAleese (succeeded Mary Robinson as president of Ireland)
- **a.** Carlow
- **b.** Mayo / Meath / Monaghan
- **c.** Sligo

3 Chlorine
- **a.** 'p'
- **b.** Two
- **c.** Five

4 Martin Scorsese
- **a.** Jupiter
- **b.** Uranus
- **c.** Saturn

5 Cosh
- **a.** Algorithm (grudgingly accept algorism which is sometimes used to mean algorithm)
- **b.** Decimal notation / the symbol for zero / zero
- **c.** Algebra (Arabic: al-jebr, reunion of broken parts)

6 First Minister of Scotland
- **a.** 'Flower of Scotland' (Scotland has no official anthem)
- **b.** South Africa (Xhosa, Zulu, Sesotho, Afrikaans and English)
- **c.** Russia (the old Soviet anthem; a lyric-free anthem had been used in the intervening years)

7 25 (joules) (KE = p^2/2m)
- **a.** Han (206 BCE–220 CE)
- **b.** Tang (618–907)
- **c.** Ming (1368–1644)

8 57 (degrees)
- **a.** (Jean) Anouilh
- **b.** (Bernard-Marie) Koltès
- **c.** *Art*

9 (Niccolo) Machiavelli
- **a.** Imperialism (Latin: imperare)
- **b.** (John A.) Hobson
- **c.** (Vladimir Ilyich) Lenin

10 Ridiculous
- **a.** (Robert Jenkinson, Earl of) Liverpool (1770–1828)
- **b.** (William) Huskisson (1770–1830)
- **c.** (George) Canning (1770–1827)

11 (Sigmund) Freud
- **a.** Nottingham
- **b.** Salford
- **c.** Leeds

12 (M.C. / Mauritz Cornelis) Escher
- **a.** Quora
- **b.** Pinterest
- **c.** Tumblr

13 1989
- **a.** (Alec) Douglas-Home (born 1903, died 1995; NB Macmillan was born in 1894 and Eden in 1897)
- **b.** (Georges) Pompidou (born 1911, died 1974; NB De Gaulle was born in 1890)
- **c.** (John F.) Kennedy (born 1917, died 1963; NB Eisenhower was born in 1890 and Truman in 1884)

14 CIVETS (Colombia, Indonesia, Vietnam, Egypt, Turkey, South Africa)
- **a.** Maryland (*Fatti maschii parole femine*)
- **b.** Minnesota
- **c.** Gold and silver

15 Bayonne
- **a.** Chipolata (Italian: *cipolla*)
- **b.** Toulouse
- **c.** Cumberland (sausage)

16 Hexagon
- **a.** (Thomas) Bowdler (*The Family Shakespeare*, 1807, 1818)
- **b.** *Henry the Fourth* part two
- **c.** (Gibbon's) *History of the Decline and Fall of the Roman Empire*

17 Gold
- **a.** (Sir) Christopher Wren
- **b.** Florin (the two-shilling piece)
- **c.** 1970s (15 February 1971)

18 Juba (the capital will eventually relocate to Ramciel)
- **a.** Endocrine (glands)
- **b.** Thyroid
- **c.** Kidneys

19 Colditz (Castle)

    a. Prisoners of war / POWs (French, in the Napoleonic Wars, and American, from the war of 1812)
    b. (The) Maze
    c. Barlinnie

20 *Roman fleuve*
    a. Era
    b. Son
    c. East (*est*, of course)

21 James I / VI (both in 1603)
    a. (Ferdinand) Magellan
    b. (Vitus) Bering
    c. (Captain James) Cook

22 *Alice's Adventures in Wonderland / Alice in Wonderland*
    a. (Miguel de) Cervantes
    b. Tenerife (the Battle of Tenerife)
    c. (Lord) Raglan (Field Marshall Fitzroy James Henry Somerset, 1788–1855, 1st Baron Raglan from 1852)

23 Utrecht
    a. Ribosome(s)
    b. Transcription
    c. Uracil

24 Sian (Sierra, India, Alpha, November)
    a. Dengue (fever)
    b. Langue (contrasted with 'parole')
    c. Harangue

25 Major-General (not 'Major' or 'General', of course; the Rule of the Major-Generals, 1655–1657)
    a. William Congreve
    b. *The Man of Mode*
    c. (Sir John) Vanbrugh

26 (Felix) Mendelssohn
    a. Feathers (the lower shaft, shaft bearing barbs, and filaments projecting from barbs respectively)
    b. Ulna
    c. Pectorals / pectoralis (accept breast muscles; not supracoracoideus muscle, which is attached to the humerus but raises the wing)

27 (Personal) pronoun (*We, It* and *She*)
    a. *The Thousand Autumns of Jacob de Zoet*
    b. *A Thousand Acres*
    c. *A Thousand Splendid Suns*

28 *Annus horribilis*
    a. Cumulus
    b. Cirrocumulus
    c. Altocumulus

29 The Royal Society (of London for Improving Natural Knowledge)
    a. British Museum
    b. James Cook / Captain Cook
    c. Kew Gardens / Royal Botanic Gardens

30 Pythagorean comma / diatonic or ditonic comma (3 to the 12 / 2 to the 19)
    a. *The Barber of Seville* by Rossini
    b. *The Elixir of Love* by Donizetti
    c. *The Magic Flute* by Mozart

Match Seven

1. Christina Rossetti's poem 'In the Bleak Midwinter' is set to the tune 'Cranham' by which English composer, who died in 1934?

Three bonus questions on weather extremes

a. Iquique, where there was no rainfall for fourteen years, and Bahía Felix, which has an average of 325 rainy days a year, are both settlements in which country?

b. In which country is Cherrapunji? Often described as 'the wettest place on Earth', it averages more than 450 inches of rain per year; the comparable figure for Manchester is 32 inches.

c. In which country is Dallol, where a mean annual temperature of over 34 degrees Celsius has been recorded?

2. In terms of given names, what seasonal pairing links the protagonist of Truman Capote's *Breakfast at Tiffany's* with the author of *Pastors and Masters* and *Parents and Children*?

Three bonus questions on botany

a. In vascular plants, what is the general name of those tissues that consist of undifferentiated cells capable of division, thereby leading to the growth of the plant?

b. Apical meristems are responsible for the primary growth of plants. Derived from the Latin for 'change', what is the general term for lateral meristems, responsible for secondary growth?

c. The outermost cambium, or phellogen, is particularly active in *Quercus suber*, an evergreen oak noted for what commercial product?

3 Answer as soon as your name is called. Give the dictionary spelling of the semi-soft Italian cheese known as 'mozzarella'.

Three bonus questions on chemistry

a. From the Latin for 'bunch', what word denotes an optically inactive mixture containing equal quantities of right and left-handed enantiomers of a chiral molecule?

b. Racemic acid is an obsolete term for an optically inactive form of which organic acid with the basic formula $C_4H_6O_6$?

c. What is the common three-word name for potassium hydrogen-tartrate, a white crystalline deposit that is an ingredient of baking powder?

4 Born in 1940, which US economist gives his name to the curve that demonstrates the theory that there is a certain point known as 'T' at which a government collects the greatest amount of taxes?

Three bonus questions on Africa. In each case, the answer is a Commonwealth member state.

a. The socialist-leaning Julius Nyerere was president of which African country from independence in 1962 until he stepped down voluntarily in 1985?

b. Kenneth Kaunda led which country to independence from Britain in 1964, and served as its president until he was voted out of office in 1991?

c. Dr Hastings Banda was the leader of which southern African country, which he governed from independence until 1994?

5 Which German composer wrote the soprano role in the 1846 oratorio *Elijah* for the Swedish singer Jenny Lind, with whom he was infatuated? He died the following year.

Three bonus questions on English history and Italian opera

a. Rossini had already used his overture to *The Barber of Seville* in an earlier opera about which Queen of England, written in 1815?

b. Produced at Milan in 1830, the opera *Anna Bolena* was the first work to achieve international recognition for which composer?

c. Premiered in Paris in 1835, Vincenzo Bellini's final opera *I Puritani* is a love story set during the time of which war?

6 What six-letter name links: a routing protocol in computer technology; a major tributary of the River Tigris; and a British army officer's personal servant? More popularly, it is the name of a costumed comic-book character created in 1939 by the artist Bob Kane and the writer Bill Finger.

Three bonus questions on names that begin and end with the same letter in each case. Simply give the name from the description.

a. A major battle fought in southern Pennsylvania in July 1863?

b. The most populous province of China?

c. A plant of genus *Panax*, cultivated, especially in East Asia, for its supposed restorative and medicinal properties?

7 Born around 1488, which Venetian artist gives his name to a gold-tinted auburn colour that features prominently in his paintings?

Three bonus questions on artists and architects born in 1599

a. Born in Antwerp in 1599, which court painter is best known for portraits of King Charles I and his family?

b. Born in 1599, Francesco Borromini is best known for baroque architecture in which city? His works include the Church of Saint Charles at the Four Fountains.

c. Born in 1599, which artist's works include *The Surrender of Breda* and *The Waterseller of Seville*?

8 What eight-letter place name links museums dedicated to William Wilberforce and Bob Marley with the starting point of Jerome K. Jerome's *Three Men in a Boat*?

Three bonus questions on novels whose titles contain a duplicated word or expression. In each case, from the description give the title of the novel and its author.

a. A novel of 1939 set in the southern USA; named after a biblical figure, its characters include Thomas Sutpen and Quentin Compson?

b. A satirical novel of 1998 that describes the creation of a giant amusement park on the Isle of Wight, based on the theme named in the title?

c. A novel about the theatre director Charles Arrowby and his rediscovered first love; it won the Booker Prize in 1978?

9 Differing by only two letters, what two names denote an Athenian statesman and lawgiver, born around 630 BC and the son and successor of King David of Israel, proverbial for his wisdom?

Three bonus questions on Israeli soldiers

a. Jailed by the British in 1939 for joining the illegal Haganah force, which defence minister was behind Israel's victory in the Six-Day War?

b. Prime minister from 1999 to 2001, who retired from the army as a lieutenant general in 1995 as the most decorated soldier in Israeli history?

c. Benjamin Netanyahu's brother Jonathan died while leading the Israeli commando rescue raid on which Ugandan airport in 1976?

10 Expressed in metres, how long is a mile? You may have 20 metres either way.

Three bonus questions on films with single-letter titles

a. Directed by Oliver Stone, which 2008 film starred Josh Brolin as the 43rd president of the USA?

b. Directed by Fritz Lang, which 1931 film starred Peter Lorre as a child murderer who becomes the object of a manhunt conducted by local criminals?

c. The work of the Greek-born director Costa-Gavras, which 1969 French film centres on the murder of a leftist politician and its subsequent investigation?

11 Indicating a state of exuberant elation, what three-word hyphenated expression is sometimes said to derive from the act of loosening a tap to allow liquor to flow freely, but may also refer to pub signs that show a male domestic fowl atop a cask or barrel?

Three bonus questions on modern board games classified as 'German-style', or 'Euro-style'

a. Created by Uwe Rosenberg in 2007, which game involves expanding from one's wooden shack by gathering resources and planting food? Its name is the Latin for 'farmer'.

b. Created by Klaus Teuber in 1995, which game involves the settling an island by newly landed seafarers, who build the board with hexagonal terrain tiles?

c. Created by Klaus-Jürgen Wrede in 2000, in which tile-laying game do players develop the area around the eponymous southern French city, noted for its medieval fortifications?

12 Which ancient city links: the first book printed in English by William Caxton; a city on the Hudson river just north of Albany; and a caddish cavalryman in Hardy's *Far from the Madding Crowd*?

Three bonus questions on writer's block

a. Following six years of creative paralysis, Amy Rosenthal wrote the play *On the Rocks* in which she alludes to the panic that writer's block induced in which New Zealand short-story writer?

b. Referring to the writer's block that plagued him, who wrote to his agent: 'I feel that this is almost too much for me,' twelve years after the publication of his first novel *Almayer's Folly*?

c. Which poet's spell of writer's block appeared to have ended by 2009 with *The Cinder Path*, his first new collection for seven years?

13 In pharmacology, for what do the letters M.L.D. stand, when indicating that measure of toxicity defined as the dose required to kill half the members of a sample population in a given time?

Three bonus questions on poisons

a. Potassium cyanide contains what two elements, in addition to potassium?

b. A molecule of the poisonous gas phosgene contains atoms of carbon, oxygen and what other element?

c. What poisonous Group 5 element is a silvery-white metalloid, and has been known by the Latin name *stibium*?

14 What two-word term is used for the lowest temperature at which the vapour of a combustible liquid can be made to ignite momentarily in air?

Three bonus questions on zoology

a. Bats belong to the order Chiroptera; the sub-order Megachiroptera comprises species of bats known by what common, general term, in reference to their diet?

b. Odonata is an order of primitive winged insects with the suborders Anisoptera, commonly known as dragonflies, and Zygoptera, known by what common name?

c. Which insectivorous mammal is the only member of the order Tubulidentata? Its common name is the Afrikaans for 'earth pig'.

15 In internet usage, for what do the letters F.T.P. stand?

Three bonus questions on European cities

a. Turku, at the mouth of the Aura river, is the oldest city and a former capital of which EU member state?

b. Trondheim, the seat of the twelfth-century Nidaros Cathedral, was a medieval capital of which country?

c. Now a major financial centre, which city on the River Main was the capital of the confederation of the Rhine from 1806 to 1815?

16 Believed to date to the early fifth century, a wooden panel on the door of the church of Santa Sabina in Rome is one of the earliest surviving depictions of which event?

Three bonus questions on an English parish church

a. Noted for its fine 'four-decker' perpendicular tower, the parish church of Mells lies five miles south-east of Midsomer Norton and Radstock, former centres of coalmining, in which English county?

b. The three-volume *Memoirs of George Sherston* and the First World War poems 'Everyone Sang' and 'The General' are works by which literary figure, who is buried in Mells churchyard?

c. The south wall of Mells church bears a memorial to Raymond, the son of which prime minister, killed during the Battle of the Somme?

17 'The American continents ... are henceforth not to be considered as subjects for future colonization by any European powers.' These are the words of which US president, in a speech of 1823?

Three bonus questions on unfortunate predictions

a. In 1774, which politician said of the American colonies, 'Four or five frigates will do the business without any military force'?

b. In a speech to western diplomats in 1956, which national leader said, 'Whether you like it or not, history is on our side. We will bury you'?

c. In 2006, which future Cabinet minister described Ireland as, 'a shining example of the art of the possible in long-term economic policymaking'?

18 What number comes next in this sequence, given in descending order: 8,128; 496; 28 and which single-digit number?

Three bonus questions on mathematics

a. Introduced by the English mathematician John Wallis in 1655, what is denoted by the mathematical symbol sometimes called the lemniscate, from the Latin for 'ribbon'?

b. In the form of a letter of the Hebrew alphabet with a subscript, what symbol is used to represent the smallest infinite cardinal number in set theory?

c. What name is given to a line that acts as the limit of a curve such that its distance from the curve approaches zero as the line tends to infinity?

19 Originally intended to be disparaging, what two-word term denotes a theoretical model of the universe which contradicted the 'steady-state' model proposed by the man who coined the term, the cosmologist Fred Hoyle, in 1950?

Three bonus questions on diagrams in physics

a. Originally believing it to represent possible evolutionary paths, the astronomer Edwin Hubble developed his 'tuning fork' diagram in 1926 to plot the morphological varieties of what objects?

b. Born in 1864, which German mathematician gives his name to a diagram that plots space along one axis and time along the other?

c. Along with Henry Norris Russell, which Danish scientist gives his name to a diagram that plots stellar type by luminosity and temperature?

20 'I yield / Upon great persuasion; and partly to save your life, / For I was told you were in a consumption.' Which of Shakespeare's heroines responds with these words to a proposal of marriage from Benedick?

Three bonus questions on lines about books in plays by Shakespeare. In each case, identify the play and the character speaking.

a.　'Knowing I loved my books, he furnished me /
From mine own library with volumes that /
I prize above my dukedom.'

b.　'I'll read enough, / When I do see the very book indeed /
Where all my sins are writ, and that's myself.'

c.　'Your face, my thane, is as a book where men /
May read strange matters.'

21 Introduced by the US cardiologists Meyer Friedman and Ray H. Rosenman in 1959, what term describes a personality type characterised by hurried activity, impatience, ambition and competitiveness?

Three bonus questions on musical centenaries

a.　2013 was the centenary of the birth of which British composer, whose first stage work was the operetta *Paul Bunyan*, to a libretto by W.H. Auden?

b.　Which German composer wrote the opera *Der Rosenkavalier*, which had its British premiere in January 1913?

c.　The premiere of which ballet by Igor Stravinsky at the Théâtre des Champs Élysées in Paris caused a riot in May 1913?

22 Originally a Tamil word for 'drummer', what term came to be applied to any casteless Hindu, hence its current usage in denoting a social outcast?

Three bonus questions on nutrition

a. The US biochemist Elmer McCollum is generally credited with the invention of the alphabetical system of naming which group of organic compounds?

b. Which letter of the alphabet is associated with the vitamin that can be described as 'anti-rachitic', or preventing the development of rickets?

c. Similarly, which letter of the alphabet is associated with the vitamin that may be described as 'anti-scorbutic'?

23 In his office at Princeton University, Albert Einstein displayed portraits of Faraday, Newton and which Scottish scientist, who gives his name to a set of four relations in thermodynamics, and a set of four equations in electromagnetism?

Three bonus questions on a name

a. Which is the largest of Neptune's moons, and is the only large satellite in the Solar System to move in a retrograde orbit?

b. A triton is a subatomic particle composed of one proton and two neutrons, and is the nucleus of tritium, a radioactive isotope of which element?

c. *Triton cristatus* is a crested species of which amphibian native to Britain?

24 Answer as soon as your name is called. How many possible four-member *University Challenge* teams can be formed from a group of seven students?

Three bonus questions on prison literature

a. 'Stone walls do not a prison make, nor iron bars a cage.' These are the opening lines of 'To Althea, from Prison', composed by which poet, who was incarcerated in Gatehouse Prison in Westminster in 1642?

b. 'Notre-Dame des Fleurs', or 'Our Lady of the Flowers', was written by which French poet, playwright and novelist during his time in Fresnes Prison in the 1940s?

c. The first part of which allegorical work was largely written while the author was imprisoned in Bedford Gaol? It was not published until 1678, some years after his release.

25 Listen carefully. What is the magnitude of the electric field inside a spherical shell of charge q and radius r?

Three bonus questions on astronomy

a. The constellation of Taurus holds two prominent star clusters whose names rhyme; give both of them.

b. The Pleiades and Hyades are both 'open' clusters, a class of objects which are young in cosmic terms, and are distinguished from which other, much older class of clusters, which includes M22 and M13?

c. What alliterative, traditional name is given to the Pleiades, referring to the number of stars visible to the naked eye on a clear night?

26 *Taking Possession of His Estate, At the Rose Tavern, Going to Court, Marrying an Old Woman, At the Gaming House, In Prison,* and *In Bedlam* are successive stages in which series of paintings of 1734 by William Hogarth?

Three bonus questions on July 1960

a. In which country was Mrs Bandaranaike elected the world's first female prime minister in July 1960?

b. Also in July 1960, shortly after the Belgian Congo declared independence, which mineral-rich province attempted to secede from the new republic?

c. Its characters including Bob Ewell and Boo Radley, which novel was first published in the USA in July 1960?

27 Of the three terms at the Universities of Oxford and Cambridge, which is the only one that has the same name at both establishments?

Three bonus questions on sport, politics and the English language

a. Concatenating the two-letter top-level domain codes of the FIFA World Cup hosts in 1998 and in 1990 gives what short English dialect word?

b. 'The Right Hon. Gentleman is afraid of an election, is he? Afraid? Frightened? Frit?' Which political figure made a memorable lapse into dialect with these words in April 1983?

c. To which senior Labour politician did Thatcher address this remark? He was chancellor of the Exchequer from 1974 to 1979.

28 An influential supporter of liberal social causes, which Hungarian-born US financier is perhaps best known for 'shorting' the pound sterling and reportedly making one billion dollars in one day when the Bank of England stopped fixing the exchange rate in 1992?

Three bonus questions on a nineteenth-century chancellor of the Exchequer

a. Described as 'a natural second-in-command', Sir Stafford Northcote served as chancellor to which prime minister from 1874 to 1880?

b. In its coverage of the 1874 general election, *The Times* had predicted, erroneously, that 'whoever is Chancellor when the Budget is produced, [it] will be abolished.' To what revenue-raising device, first introduced in 1799, was it referring?

c. In 1878, Northcote raised income tax to five pence in the pound, following increased expenditure on military preparations against which country?

29 *Signs and Wonders* is a 425-piece installation in the uppermost cupola of the V&A by which British ceramic artist, who wrote the best-selling 2010 family biography *The Hare with Amber Eyes*?

Three bonus questions on prominent people who give their names to stations of the Paris Métro. In each case, name the person from the description.

a. A republican statesman of Italian ancestry who directed the defence of Paris during the Franco-Prussian war and helped to found the Third Republic?

b. A general often credited with bringing about the Allied victory at the Battle of the Marne in 1914? This included commandeering taxicabs to take troops to the front.

c. A major figure of the Romantic movement in France, the author of *Cromwell* and *Notre Dame de Paris*?

30 Listen carefully and answer as soon as your name is called. If a ball is cast straight up at twenty metres per second and the acceleration due to gravity is ten metres per second squared, then what is the maximum height of the ball?

Three bonus questions on geometry

a. In geometry, what term describes a topological space each point of which has a neighbourhood homeomorphic to the interior of a sphere in a Euclidean space of fixed dimension?

b. Named after its discoverer, which closed two-dimensional smooth manifold can be realised in four dimensions as a bottle whose inside and outside coincide?

c. If the Klein bottle is cut in half down its length, two copies of which one-sided surface result, formed by half-twisting a rectangular length of material and joining the ends?

> 'What you want from an appearance on *University Challenge* is a nation open-mouthed with awe at your extraordinary knowledge, insight and intellect. But the reality is a nation of people thinking "I can't believe he didn't know that."'
>
> DAVID NICHOLLS
> Author, *Starter for Ten*

The Answers

1 (Gustav) Holst
   a. Chile
   b. India (some places in the Highlands, Cumbria and Snowdonia get around 100 inches)
   c. Ethiopia

2 Holly and Ivy (Golightly and Compton-Burnett, of course)
   a. Meristems
   b. Cambium (Latin: *cambium*)
   c. Cork

3 M.o.z.z.a.r.e.l.l.a.
   a. Racemic (mixture) (Latin: *racemus*)
   b. Tartaric (acid; accept 2,3-dihydroxybutanedioic acid / tartrate)
   c. Cream of tartar

4 (Arthur) Laffer
   a. Tanzania
   b. Zambia
   c. Malawi

5 (Felix) Mendelssohn
   a. Elizabeth (*Elisabetta, Regina d'Inghilterra*; also used previously for his opera *Aureliano in Palmira*, 1813)
   b. (Gaetano) Donizetti
   c. English Civil War

⑥ Batman
    a. Gettysburg
    b. Guangdong (NB the older name of Canton was used only for the province's capital, Guangzhou, not the province itself)
    c. Ginseng

⑦ Titian
    a. (Antony) van Dyck
    b. Rome
    c. (Diego) Velázquez

⑧ Kingston (upon Hull, Jamaica and upon Thames, of course)
    a. *Absalom, Absalom!* by (William) Faulkner
    b. *England, England* by Julian Barnes
    c. *The Sea, the Sea* by Iris Murdoch

⑨ Solon and Solomon
    a. Moshe Dayan
    b. Ehud Barak
    c. Entebbe

⑩ 1609 (so accept 1589–1629)
    a. *W* (George W. Bush, of course)
    b. *M*
    c. *Z*

⑪ Cock-a-hoop
    a. Agricola
    b. The Settlers of Catan
    c. Carcassonne

⑫ Troy (*Recuyell of the Histories of*; Sergeant)
    a. Katherine Mansfield (Amy is daughter of the late Jack Rosenthal; the play was first performed in 2008)
    b. Joseph Conrad

    c.   (Sir) Andrew Motion

13 Median Lethal Dose
    a.   Carbon and nitrogen (formula: KCn)
    b.   Chlorine (phosgene formula: $COCl_2$)
    c.   Antimony

14 Flash point (not auto-ignition temperature, which does not require an ignition source; not kindling point or fire point)
    a.   Fruit bats (also known as flying foxes and megabats, but these do not answer the question)
    b.   Damselflies
    c.   Aardvark

15 File Transfer Protocol
    a.   Finland
    b.   Norway
    c.   Gothenburg

16 The Crucifixion (of Jesus, who is shown standing between the two thieves, palms nailed to the uprights of T-shaped structures)
    a.   Somerset
    b.   (Siegfried) Sassoon
    c.   Asquith (the Asquith family still owns the manor house nearby)

17 (James) Monroe (the first expression of what became the Monroe Doctrine)
    a.   (Lord) North (Frederick North, 2nd Earl of Guilford, Prime Minister 1770–1782)
    b.   (Nikita) Khrushchev
    c.   (George) Osborne (two years later, Ireland was the first EU country officially to enter a recession)

18 6 (perfect numbers: each is the exact sum of its positive divisors)
    a.   Infinity (i.e. ∞)
    b.   Aleph-null / aleph-naught / aleph-zero

    c.   Asymptote

19 Big Bang
    a.   Galaxies
    b.   (Hermann) Minkowski (1864–1909)
    c.   (Ejnar) Hertzsprung (1873–1967)

20 Beatrice (in *Much Ado about Nothing*)
    a.   *The Tempest* – Prospero
    b.   *Richard the Second* – Richard II
    c.   *Macbeth* – Lady Macbeth

21 Type A (whereas Type B doesn't mind losing)
    a.   Benjamin Britten
    b.   Richard Strauss (if they answer just 'Strauss', prompt for more, of course)
    c.   *The Rite of Spring*

22 Pariah
    a.   Vitamins (Elmer Verner McCollum, 1879–1967)
    b.   D
    c.   C (preventing the development of scurvy)

23 (James Clerk) Maxwell (1831–1879)
    a.   Triton
    b.   Hydrogen
    c.   Newt / aquatic salamander

24 Thirty-five (working: the number of ways of choosing r elements from an n element set is the binomial coefficient 'n choose r' = $n!/(r!(n-r)!)$. We have $7!/(4!3!) = (7 \times 6 \times 5)/(3 \times 2 \times 1) = 7 \times 5 = 35$)
    a.   Richard Lovelace
    b.   Jean Genet
    c.   *The Pilgrim's Progress* (by Bunyan, of course)

25 Zero (because of Gauss' law)

    a. Pleiades and Hyades
    b. Globular (clusters)
    c. The Seven Sisters

26 *A Rake's Progress*
    a. Sri Lanka (accept Ceylon, as it was then known)
    b. Katanga
    c. *To Kill a Mockingbird*

27 Michaelmas (Oxford: Michaelmas, Hilary, Trinity; Cambridge: Michaelmas, Lent, Easter)
    a. Frit (France and Italy)
    b. Margaret Thatcher
    c. (Denis) Healey

28 George Soros
    a. Disraeli
    b. Income tax
    c. Russia

29 (Edmund) de Waal (b. 1964)
    a. (Léon) Gambetta (1838–1882)
    b. (Joseph Simon) Gallieni (1849–1916)
    c. (Victor) Hugo (1802–1885)

30 Twenty metres
    a. Manifold
    b. Klein bottle (Felix Klein, 1849–1925)
    c. Möbius strip (August Möbius, 1790–1868)

Match Eight

1. Quote: 'Recipient of an astonishing amount of romantic historical attention, [she] impresses by her talent for wasting all the considerable assets that came her way. The ability to produce beautiful needlework is no basis for government.' These words describe which British monarch, executed in 1587?

Three bonus questions on Swedish scientists

   a. Which Swedish scientist gives his name to the unit of length that is one times ten to the minus ten metres?

   b. Born in 1859, which Swedish scientist gives his name to an equation linking the rate constant of a chemical reaction to its activation energy?

   c. Born in 1707, which Swedish scientist brought into general use the binomial system of classifying plants and animals?

2. Which five-letter word is composed of two personal pronouns: the first person plural objective, followed by the third person singular feminine objective?

Three bonus questions on a novel

   a. In which French novel of 1848 is the heroine described as attending the theatre always accompanied by three things: her opera-glass, a bag of sweets, and a bouquet of the flowers, either red or white, which give her the name by which she is often known?

b. Which choreographer created the 1963 ballet *Marguerite and Armand*, based on *La Dame aux camélias*?

c. Ashton created Marguerite and Armand for the new partnership of Margot Fonteyn and which other dancer at the Royal Ballet?

3 Telling the story of Frank and April Wheeler's failing marriage, which novel of 1961 by the US writer Richard Yates was adapted into a film of 2008 starring Kate Winslet and Leonardo DiCaprio?

Three bonus questions on physical principles

a. Which physical principle asserts the equality of inertial and gravitational acceleration of mass, and implies that acceleration under gravity is independent of the nature of the body?

b. The principle that a ray of light will follow the path that takes the least time is attributed to which seventeenth-century French mathematician?

c. Which Austrian physicist gives his name to the exclusion principle of quantum mechanics, which states that no two identical fermions can occupy the same quantum state?

4 In French history, which polity is generally held to have begun in 1870 and to have ended in 1940?

Three bonus questions on foreign secretaries, in the words of the Foreign and Commonwealth Office website. In each case, name the Labour prime minister in whose Cabinet the following served.

a. 'Patrick Gordon Walker ... A good linguist, he was one of the few British foreign secretaries this century who could converse in German with a German foreign minister.'

b. 'Arthur Henderson ... Known affectionately as "Uncle Arthur", he was a teetotaller, a non-smoker and a Methodist lay preacher; an unusual combination in the Foreign Office.'

c. 'Herbert Morrison ... did not quite have a diplomatic touch: he once joked, "Foreign policy would be okay except for the bloody foreigners."'

5 Listen carefully. If the sixteen states of Germany are arranged alphabetically by their English names, which comes second?

Three bonus questions on mountains

a. On which large island is Puncak Jaya, also known as Carstensz Pyramid? 4,884 metres in height, it is the highest point between the Himalayas and the Andes, and the highest island peak in the world.

b. On which island is Mauna Kea, the second highest island peak?

c. Finally, on which large island is Mount Kinabalu, just over 4,000 metres in height?

6 Meaning 'a source of evil' or 'a poison', what short word is found in the common name of the plant *Aconitum lycoctonum*, thought to deter wolves, and the composite plants *erigeron* and *pulicaria*, whose strong smell is said to drive away fleas?

Three bonus questions on ISO 4217 international currency abbreviations, specifically, those that spell words. For example, the abbreviation for the Cuban peso spells the word 'cup'. In each case, give the country and currency whose abbreviation corresponds to the following.

a. To apply with friction or pressure, for example ointment or sun cream?

b. A 1969 film directed by Ken Loach; set in a mining village, it tells of a troubled young boy and a bird of prey?

c. A man who behaves dishonourably towards women?

7 Palynology is the analysis of the structure and dispersal of which particular spores, regarded as indicators of plant taxonomy and distribution, and causative agents of allergic reactions?

Three bonus questions on roses

a. 'Gather ye rosebuds while ye may, / Old time is still a-flying: / And this same flower that smiles to-day, / To-morrow will be dying.' Who wrote these words in a poem of 1648, part of the collection known as *Hesperides*?

b. 'The rainbow comes and goes, / And lovely is the rose.' Which Romantic poet wrote these words?

c. 'Treaties, you see, are like girls and roses: they last while they last.' Who made this statement in a speech at the Elysée Palace in 1963?

8 Lady Augusta Gregory and W.B. Yeats were the among the early directors of which theatre, the home of the Irish National Theatre Society, which opened in Dublin in 1904?

Three bonus questions on national theatres

a. The Abbey Theatre was the scene of a riot among members of the audience for the premiere in 1907 of *The Playboy of the Western World* by which Irish playwright?

b. The National Theatre of Wales launched in 2009, since when its programme has included *The Passion*, staged in Port Talbot and starring which actor, born there in 1969?

c. In which London theatre was the National Theatre of Great Britain founded in 1963? It was based there until it moved to its new home on the South Bank in 1976.

9 Anzio, Backley, Colombo and Dorking are the first four of twenty-six places mentioned in the titles of chapters of which novel of 1992 by Sebastian Faulks?

Three bonus questions on similar words. In each case, give the word from the description. All three answers end in the same four letters.

a. The common name of the shrub *Lawsonia inermis*? Its leaves yield a dye used to create temporary tattoos and to colour hair.

b. A genus of leguminous plants; some species bear seed pods that are used as a laxative?

c. The abode of the damned in Jewish and Christian eschatology; its name comes from a valley near Jerusalem where children were burned as sacrifices to pagan gods?

10 Used in bronzing and in preparing imitation gold leaf, 'Dutch metal' is an alloy consisting largely of copper with which other metal?

Three bonus questions on a chemical element

a. Heavy spar and witherite are among the main ores of which chemical element in Group 2 of the Periodic Table? It is found naturally only in combination with other elements.

b. Compounds of barium, particularly barium nitrate, have been used in fireworks to impart what colour to the flames?

c. Which opaque compound of barium is used as a 'meal' before a medical X-ray, usually of the upper gastro-intestinal tract?

11 Upon attending the 2008 party convention in Denver, Mordecai was claimed to be the first official live mascot in the history of the Democratic party. What type of animal was it?

Three bonus questions on nineteenth-century US presidents

a. After his second term in office, which president went on a highly publicised world tour, meeting Bismarck and Queen Victoria? His tomb in New York is one of the largest mausoleums in the world.

b. Which president survived an impeachment and later became the only former president to serve in the Senate, when he was elected for Tennessee?

c. In retirement, which president surveyed and designed the University of Virginia at Charlottesville, not far from his home at Monticello?

12 The revolutionary socialist league formed in Germany during the First World War by Karl Liebknecht and Rosa Luxemburg later became the German Communist Party, and was named after which Thracian gladiator who led a slave revolt against Rome in 73 BC?

Three bonus questions on a shared surname

a. *A Financial History of the World* and *History's Age of Hatred* are subtitles of works by which historian, born in 1964?

b. Born in County Down in 1884, Harry Ferguson was an industrialist best known for his innovations in which broad field of automotive engineering?

c. Which club did Sir Alex Ferguson manage from 1978 to 1986, during which time they won the European Cup Winners' Cup once and the Scottish League three times?

13 Meaning 'in the chapel style', what term evolved in the nineteenth century to signify performance in the style of the Papal Chapel, in other words without instrumental support, and is now used generally for unaccompanied singing?

Three bonus questions on the New York Times's 10 best books of 2011

a. Spanning such topics as waterboarding, Henry VIII and Harry Potter, *Arguably* is an essay collection by which author, journalist and polemicist, who died in December 2011?

b. Given the UK subtitle *An Epic History of Two Nations Divided*, Amanda Foreman's book *A World on Fire* is about Britain's role in which war?

c. Manning Marable's work subtitled *A Life of Reinvention* is a biography of which African American, a leader of the Nation of Islam, who was assassinated in 1965?

14 In the Oxford Dictionary of English, the words 'duumvirate' and 'duvet' come immediately before and after the surname of which two former Haitian dictators, a father and son known as 'Papa Doc' and 'Baby Doc' respectively?

Three bonus questions on the Caribbean

a. Now known as the Virgin Islands of the United States, the Caribbean islands of St Thomas, St John and St Croix were purchased by the USA from which country in 1917?

b. 300 kilometres east of Puerto Rico, the island of St Martin is one of the smallest sea islands to be divided between two countries. Which two countries are they?

c. Which Caribbean country was claimed by Christopher Columbus in 1492, and remained under Spanish control for more than four hundred years?

15 Which principality and its inhabitants are denoted by the term 'Monegasque'?

Three bonus questions on the architect Frank Gehry

a. Co-designed with Vlado Milunic, the so-called Dancing House in Prague is also known by the name of which American duo?

b. Der Neue Zollhof consists of three buildings in close proximity on the riverfront of which city, the capital of North Rhine Westphalia?

c. Completed in 2003, which Gehry-designed Los Angeles concert hall is named after the recipient of fifty-nine Oscar nominations?

16 'If there were a verb meaning "to believe falsely", it would not have any significant first-person, present indicative.' These are the words of which Austrian-born philosopher, in the 1953 work *Philosophical Investigations*?

> **Three bonus questions on Africa. In each case, name the country from the list of those it borders.**
>
> **a.** First: Namibia, South Africa, Zambia and Zimbabwe?
>
> **b.** Burkina Faso, Niger, Nigeria and Togo?
>
> **c.** And finally: Eritrea, Ethiopia and Somalia?

17 Thought to date to around 1500 BCE, the earliest form of which Indo-European language is known as 'Vedic', and its most common register as 'Classical'? It is one of twenty-two 'scheduled languages' in the constitution of India.

> **Three bonus questions on historic routes**
>
> **a.** Described as 'Britain's oldest road', which national trail runs from Ivinghoe Beacon in Buckinghamshire to Overton Hill in Wiltshire?
>
> **b.** Thought by some to have been a branch of the Icknield Way, the Peddar's Way follows the route of a Roman road for 46 miles to the north coast of which county?
>
> **c.** The Pilgrims' Way is a historic route that runs from Winchester to the shrine of Saint Thomas à Becket in which city?

18 Meaning a dangerous or unstable situation, or a key turning-point, what six-letter word derives ultimately from the Greek verb 'to decide'?

Three bonus questions on geology

a. Igneous rocks are classified as acid or basic, according to the level of what compound within them?

b. Igneous rocks formed at depth are called plutonic, while those formed at the surface are called volcanic. What term denotes those rocks formed in between?

c. Which potassium-rich feldspar, found in igneous rocks, usually occurs as white or pink crystals and has a name derived from the Greek for 'straight' and 'breaking'?

19 Which sport was first recognised by the International Olympic Committee in 1994 and made its Winter Games debut four years later with the 'Giant Slalom' and the 'Half-Pipe' events?

Three bonus questions on the human brain

a. Also known as the 'grey matter' and rich in synapses, what two-word term denotes the much-folded outer layer of the cerebral hemispheres?

b. Which human function is associated with Broca's area and Wernicke's area of the cerebral cortex?

c. What term denotes the enlargement of the hindbrain, anterior to the medulla oblongata? It coordinates and regulates motor activity.

20 *Orion, Falcon, Antares, Intrepid* and *Eagle* were the names of what precise type of spacecraft, employed by NASA between 1969 and 1972?

Three bonus questions on a planet of the Solar System

a. Which planet has two large highland regions named after the goddesses Ishtar and Aphrodite, along with other surface features named Helen, Guinevere and Lavinia?

b. A many-ringed impact crater in the southern hemisphere of Venus is named after which Austrian physicist? She was involved in the discovery and explanation of nuclear fission, and gives her name to the element with the atomic number 109.

c. A lowland area in the northern hemisphere is named after which Inuit goddess? She also gives her name to one of the most distant bodies known in the Solar System, discovered in 2003.

21 Listen carefully and answer as soon as your name is called. When rolling two fair six-sided dice, what is the probability that their scores add together to make four?

Three bonus questions on mathematical group theory

a. What six-letter term describes a group all of whose members are powers of a given element when written multiplicatively, for example the integers modulo n?

b. Which type of group contains no proper non-trivial normal sub-groups, the classification of all such finite groups being a major achievement of twentieth-century mathematics?

c. Named after the Norwegian mathematician who helped develop their theory, which type of group possesses a commutative binary operation, so that ab equals ba for all a and b?

22 The process in which bubbles of vapour are formed due to the saturated vapour pressure of a liquid being equal to the external pressure, usually due to the presence of heat, is known by what common term?

Three bonus questions on soya

a. A thick paste used for sauces and soups, which Japanese seasoning is made by fermenting rice or barley and soya beans with salt and the fungus known as koji?

b. Including soy sauce and mature cheeses, what Japanese word is used for the category of taste corresponding to the 'savoury' flavour of free glutamates in various foods?

c. What Japanese word, literally meaning 'glaze grill', is given to a dish consisting of fish or meat marinated in soy sauce and grilled?

23 Which English composer wrote the cantata *Saint Nicholas*, with a text by Eric Crozier, for the centennial celebrations of Lancing College in Sussex in 1948? It was also performed in June of that year at the first Aldeburgh Festival.

Three bonus questions on fictional characters

a. Queequeg, a Polynesian prince-turned-whaler, who both eats and shaves with his harpoon, is a character in which novel of 1851?

b. Daniel Quilp, described as being 'so low in stature as to be quite a dwarf, though his head and face were large enough for the body of a giant', appears in which novel by Charles Dickens?

c. Mister Quelch is the form master of the Remove at Greyfriars School in a series of books by Frank Richards about which eponymous character?

24 Answer as soon as your name is called. Give the dictionary spelling of the word 'quaff', meaning 'drink heartily'.

Three bonus questions on infections

a. 'Mycosis', 'candidiasis' and 'tinea pedis' all belong to what general class of infection?

b. 'Impetigo' and 'cellulitis' are bacterial infections affecting which part of the body?

c. Meaning 'secret', what term denotes a hidden infection first recognised by secondary manifestations?

25 'Xmas and Christmas: A Lost Chapter from Herodotus' is a satirical essay in the posthumous 1970 collection *God in the Dock* by which novelist and Christian apologist?

Three bonus questions on power

a. 'Every communist must grasp the truth: "Political power grows out of the barrel of a gun."' Later the leader of his country, which revolutionary made this statement in 1938?

b. 'The greater the power, the more dangerous the abuse.' Which political figure said this in his 1771 'Speech on the Middlesex Election'?

c. 'Power is not a means, it is an end. One does not establish a dictatorship in order to safeguard a revolution; one makes the revolution in order to establish the dictatorship.' These words appear in which fictional work, first published in 1949?

26 In biology, which Greek word meaning 'virgin birth' is used when an egg grows and develops without being fertilised by sperm, a phenomenon which allows normally sexual species to reproduce asexually?

Three bonus questions on vertebrate bone structure

a. From the Greek meaning 'growing through', what term denotes the mid-section or shaft of long-limb bones? In adults their central medullary cavities are filled with yellow marrow.

b. What term denotes the expanded ends of limb bones? They contain red marrow and articulate with adjacent bones to form joints.

c. What connective tissue forms the smooth articulating surface of the epiphyses of long bones?

27 In his 2010 work *Bounce: The Myth of Talent and the Power of Practice*, the British journalist Matthew Syed draws on his experiences as a leading international competitor in which Olympic sport?

Three bonus questions on games and sports

a. What game links 'The Stranger Song' by Leonard Cohen, the 1998 film *Rounders*, and Victoria Coren's book *For Richer or Poorer*?

b. What sport links Shakespeare's *Henry the Fifth*, a pivotal moment of the French revolution depicted in a work by David, and Alfred Hitchcock's film *Strangers on a Train*?

c. What game links Matt Charman's play *The Machine*, Vladimir Nabokov's 1964 novel *The Defence*, and the second part of Eliot's *The Waste Land*?

28 Published posthumously in 1955, *A Child's Christmas in Wales* is a prose recollection by which writer? His earlier works included *The Map of Love* and *Portrait of the Artist as a Young Dog.*

Three bonus questions on bells

a. Inscribed with a verse from the book of Leviticus, the bell in Philadelphia that was heard at the first public reading of the US Declaration of Independence is commonly known by what name?

b. Weighing approximately 24,000 kilograms, the St Peter's Bell, or 'Fat Peter', is the largest in which German cathedral, close to the River Rhine?

c. The cracked 'Tsar Bell', also known as the 'Tsar Kolokol', is a giant bell that stands in the grounds of which building complex?

29 Which Scottish island comes next in this sequence, given in descending order by area: Lewis and Harris; Skye; Shetland mainland; and... what?

Three bonus questions on twentieth-century literature

a. Referring to the generation of American writers prominent in the 1920s and disillusioned by the First World War, what two-word term was used by Ernest Hemingway in an epigraph to *The Sun Also Rises*?

b. *Blood Wedding* and *The House of Bernarda Alba* are plays by which member of the group of Spanish writers known as the 'Generation of 1927'?

c. A term usually credited to Jack Kerouac, US authors including Allen Ginsberg and William Burroughs are often described as members of what 'generation'?

30 Leoneg, Tregerieg and Gwenedeg are among varieties of which Western European language? Lacking official or regional status, it is closely related to Cornish.

Three bonus questions linked by a name

a. What is the surname of the Irish poet who chose the title of his 1930 autobiography, *To Return to All That*, in response to a book written by his son the previous year?

b. Richard Graves's 1779 novel *Columella* was inspired by the life of which contemporary writer? His works include *The Schoolmistress* and *Essays on Men and Manners*.

c. Named after an Irish physician, Graves' disease causes an enlargement of which gland in the human body?

> 'I loved the sense of excitement and the notion of being able to busk it and get though it on sheer gutsiness and imagination. I loved all of that, and it may have been in black and white, and I may have been wearing a dreadful suit, but I felt this was me. This was where I belonged.'
>
> JOHN SIMPSON
> (BBC World Affairs Editor)
> Contestant, 1965

The Answers

1 Mary, Queen of Scots (described in *Who's Who in British History*)
- **a.** (Anders Jonas) Ångström (1814–1874)
- **b.** (Svante August) Arrhenius (1859–1927; the Arrhenius equation)
- **c.** (Carl / Carolus) Linnaeus (1707–1778)

2 Usher
- **a.** *La Dame aux camélias / The Lady of the Camellias* (Dumas, fils)
- **b.** (Sir) Frederick Ashton
- **c.** Rudolf Nureyev

3 *Revolutionary Road*
- **a.** (Principle of) equivalence (three forms in current use: weak or Galilean or universality of free fall; Einsteinian; and strong)
- **b.** (Pierre de) Fermat (c.1610–1665)
- **c.** (Wolfgang) Pauli (1900–1958)

4 The Third Republic
- **a.** (Harold) Wilson (served 1964–1965; was Secretary for Commonwealth Relations under Attlee)
- **b.** (Ramsay) Macdonald (served 1929–1931; was President of the Board of Education in Asquith's wartime coalition Cabinet, also Minister without Portfolio under Lloyd George)
- **c.** (Clement) Attlee (served 1951; Supply Minister, later Home Secretary, in Churchill's wartime Cabinet)

5 Bavaria (Baden-Wurttemberg is first)
- **a.** New Guinea (older estimates say 5,030 metres; NB not Papua New Guinea, which is not the name of the island, and the peak lies within Indonesian territory)
- **b.** Hawaii / 'Big Island'
- **c.** Borneo (Malaysia)

6 Bane (wolfbane / wolfsbane, fleabane)
- **a.** Russian ruble (i.e. 'Rub')
- **b.** Kenyan shilling (i.e. 'Kes')
- **c.** Canadian dollar (i.e. 'Cad')

7 Pollen (grains)
- **a.** (Robert) Herrick (1591–1674)
- **b.** Wordsworth ('Ode, Intimations of Immortality')
- **c.** (Charles) de Gaulle

8 Abbey Theatre
- **a.** J.M. Synge (John Millington Synge, 1871–1909)
- **b.** Michael Sheen (who also co-directed)
- **c.** The Old Vic

9 *A Fool's Alphabet*
- **a.** Henna
- **b.** Senna
- **c.** Gehenna

10 Zinc (copper 84 per cent; zinc 16 per cent)
- **a.** Barium (barite is its principal ore)
- **b.** Green
- **c.** Barium sulphate

11 A donkey
- **a.** (Ulysses S.) Grant (President 1869–1877)
- **b.** (Andrew) Johnson (President 1865–1869; impeached in the House; Senator for Tennessee, 1857–62 and 1875)

c.   (Thomas) Jefferson (President 1801–1809)

12 Spartacus (the Spartacus league / Spartakists)
      a.   Niall Ferguson (*The Ascent of Money* and *The War of the World*)
      b.   Farm / agricultural machinery (accept tractors or similar)
      c.   Aberdeen

13 A cappella / alla capella
      a.   Christopher Hitchens
      b.   American Civil War
      c.   Malcolm X (born Malcolm Little; later El-Hajj Malik el-Shabazz)

14 Duvalier (François, 1907–1971 and Jean-Claude, 1951–2014, the latter overthrown in 1986)
      a.   Denmark
      b.   France and the Netherlands
      c.   Cuba

15 Monaco
      a.   Fred and Ginger / Fred Astaire and Ginger Rogers (officially, it is the Nationale-Nederlanden building)
      b.   Düsseldorf
      c.   Walt Disney

16 (Ludwig) Wittgenstein
      a.   Botswana
      b.   Benin
      c.   Djibouti

17 Sanskrit
      a.   Ridgeway
      b.   Norfolk
      c.   Canterbury

18 Crisis (Greek: *krinein*)
- **a.** Silica or silicon dioxide (acid igneous rocks contain more than 66 per cent of silica by weight)
- **b.** Hypabyssal
- **c.** Orthoclase

19 Snowboard(ing)
- **a.** Cerebral cortex
- **b.** Speech / language
- **c.** Cerebellum

20 Lunar modules / lunar landing modules / (Apollo) Moon landing modules
- **a.** Venus
- **b.** (Lise) Meitner (Meitnerium)
- **c.** Sedna

21 One in twelve
- **a.** Cyclic
- **b.** Simple groups
- **c.** Abelian (after Niels Henrik Abel, 1802–1829)

22 Boiling
- **a.** Miso
- **b.** Umami
- **c.** Teriyaki

23 (Benjamin) Britten
- **a.** *Moby-Dick* (*: or, The Whale*)
- **b.** *The Old Curiosity Shop*
- **c.** Billy Bunter

24 Q.u.a.f.f.
- **a.** Fungal
- **b.** Skin
- **c.** Occult

25 C.S. Lewis
- **a.** Mao Zedong / Mao Tse-Tung
- **b.** Edmund) Burke
- **c.** *Nineteen Eighty-Four*

26 Parthenogenesis
- **a.** Diaphysis (Greek: *dia*, 'through', phusis, 'growth'; it is also known as 'centrum', but this doesn't answer the etymology)
- **b.** Epiphysis / epiphyses
- **c.** Cartilage

27 Table tennis
- **a.** Poker ('the holy game of poker'; John Dahl's film; she is a professional poker player)
- **b.** Tennis (the gift of tennis balls; the Tennis Court Oath; player Guy Haines)
- **c.** Chess (Kasparov v Deep Blue; aka The Luzhin Defence; 'A Game of Chess')

28 Dylan Thomas
- **a.** The Liberty Bell (Leviticus 25:10: 'Proclaim liberty throughout all the land unto all the inhabitants thereof')
- **b.** Cologne (Cathedral / the High Cathedral of Saints Peter and Mary)
- **c.** (Moscow) Kremlin

29 Mull (Islay and Orkney mainland come next)
- **a.** Lost generation ('"You are all a lost generation." – Gertrude Stein in conversation')
- **b.** (Federico Garcia) Lorca
- **c.** Beat generation / Beats

30 Breton

a. Graves (Alfred Perceval, responding to Robert Graves's 1929 *Goodbye to All That*)
b. (William) Shenstone
c. Thyroid (gland)

Match Nine

1 What final two letters link words meaning 'European who amassed a fortune with the East India Company', 'chocolate substitute made from the fruit of the locust tree' and 'giant spider in the *Lord of the Rings* trilogy?

> **Three bonus questions on *The World's Wife*, a series of poems by Carol Ann Duffy in which she writes in the imagined voices of the wives of historical characters. In each case, identify the historical figure whose wife has the following lines.**
>
> **a.** '7 April 1852. / Went to the zoo / I said to him – / Something about that chimp over there reminds / Me of you.'
>
> **b.** 'He lived. I saw the horror on his face, / I heard his mother's crazy song. I breathed / His stench; my bridegroom in his rotting shroud.'
>
> **c.** 'My living laughing love – / I hold him in the casket of my widow's head / As he held me upon that next best bed.'

2 Choledocholithiasis is a medical condition caused by the presence of what objects in the bile duct?

Three bonus questions on medicine. In each case, give the arthropod vectors of the following infectious diseases.

a. Bubonic plague is caused by the bacterium *Yersinia pestis*. What insect is responsible for carrying it from its reservoir in rats to humans?

b. Lyme disease is caused by species of Borellia. What small arachnids transmit the bacteria from their rodent hosts to humans?

c. Which large fly acts as both host and vector of *Trypanosoma brucei*, causing African sleeping sickness in humans?

3 What short word is spelt using the middle initials of the Civil Rights activist Susan Anthony, the Confederate General Robert Lee, and John Rockefeller, the founder of the Standard Oil Company?

Three bonus questions on palindromes

a. Which musical note has a five-letter palindromic name derived from a Latin word meaning 'smallest'?

b. What short palindrome can mean both the seed of a fruit and an item of military insignia found, for example, on the shoulder of an army lieutenant's uniform?

c. What is the nine-letter palindromic name of the official language of the Indian state of Kerala?

4 In ecology, what term denotes the frame used to isolate a measured area, usually a one-metre or a quarter-metre square, in order to sample a community of plants or slow-moving animals?

Three bonus questions on botany

a. Name all three of the structures that form the carpel of a typical angiosperm.

b. After fertilisation, which part of the carpel develops into the pericarp of the fruit?

c. What short term denotes a dry indihiscent fruit, usually containing a single seed with lignified pericarp?

5 The basilar membrane, the tectorial membrane and Reissner's membrane are all found in which vertebrate sensory organ?

Three bonus questions on word pairs. The second word in each case is formed by adding the letter 'o' to the end of the first, for example 'concert' and 'concerto'. In each case, give both words from the definitions.

a. 'Large branch of a tree' and 'unsatisfactory place of consignment or oblivion'?

b. 'Prudishly disapproving' and 'variety of summer cabbage'?

c. 'Sudden rush of wind' and 'enjoyment and enthusiasm in doing something'?

6 What technique utilises the interference between two parts of a split laser beam to produce a photographic image without a lens? It was invented by the Hungarian-born physicist Dennis Gabor.

Three bonus questions on classical terms and their anagrams. In each case, give both words from the explanation or definition.

a. 'Relating to a Greek philosopher who died in 399 BC' and 'a composition in which, for example, the initial letters in each line together form a word'?

b. 'The intricate knot that Alexander the Great cut through with a sword' and 'loving and respecting to the point of worship'?

c. 'The cognomen of the Latin prose author Petronius' and 'a dish of toasted cheese, often associated with Wales'?

7 Identify the poet who wrote these lines: 'The mind is its own place, and in itself / Can make a Heav'n of Hell, a Hell of Heav'n.'

Three bonus questions on literature and alcohol

a. 'Alcohol is seldom far from the reach of [his] characters, and its influence was clearly some kind of daemon … in his life.' Proposing 'Whisky fictions' as a sub-category of his work, these words of Christopher Hitchens refer to which British novelist, born in 1904?

b. 'Is this my milieu where I must / How Graham-Greeneish! How infra dig! / Snatch from the bottle in my bag / An analeptic swig?' These lines are from 'On the Circuit', a 1963 work by which English poet?

c. According to urbandictionary.com, the name of which US novelist and Nobel laureate may be used verbally to mean 'writing a paper under the influence of alcohol'?

8 Developed in the 1950s and generally indicated by a single six-letter word, what is the principal worldwide system of transcribing Chinese characters into Roman script?

Three bonus questions on French detectives. In each case, I want the surname of the fictional character described and his creator.

a. A character who made his first appearance in the 1841 short story 'Murders in the Rue Morgue', before the word 'detective' existed; his surname relates to a pine tree or trees?

b. A detective who appeared in more than seventy novels from 1931 to 1972; his surname means 'thin person'?

c. A detective who made his first appearance in a film of 1963; the two elements of his surname mean 'nail' and 'bucket'?

9 From words meaning 'do everything', what Latin-derived term denotes a person with many diverse responsibilities? It appears memorably in an aria sung by Figaro at his first entrance in Rossini's *The Barber of Seville*.

Three bonus questions on a footballer

a. Consisting of three statues depicting him at various stages of his career, a memorial to which footballer stands outside the Britannia Stadium in Stoke-on-Trent? Known as 'the Wizard of Dribble', he died in 2000.

b. At what age did Matthews play his last professional match, for Stoke City against Fulham in the First Division in 1965? You may have one year either way.

c. With which club did Matthews win the FA Cup in 1953, a match often known as the 'Matthews Final'?

10 Quote: 'We hear from America and the continent all sorts of disagreeable things about England – the unmusical, anti-artistic, unphilosophic country. We quite agree.' These words appeared in 1914 in the manifesto issued by which group of artists and writers?

Three bonus questions on philosophy and literature

a. Which Latin-derived philosophical term was popularised by Turgenev's 1862 novel *Fathers and Sons*, where it was used to describe the crude scientism espoused by the character Bazarov?

b. The anarchist Sergey Nechayev became the model for a self-described nihilist in *The Possessed*, sometimes called *The Devils*, a novel of 1872 by which Russian writer?

c. Written in 1880, *Vera; or, The Nihilists* was the first stage work of which Irish literary figure?

11 What geographical feature links 'Einstein', 'Dover' and 'Chesil' in the titles of works by Philip Glass, Matthew Arnold and Ian McEwan?

Three bonus questions on game designers

a. Known as 'the father of computer gaming', which creator of so-called 'god games' is noted for the *Civilization* and *Railroad Tycoon* series?

b. Called 'the father of modern video games', which Japanese designer is the creator of Nintendo's *Super Mario Bros*, *Donkey Kong* and *Legend of Zelda* franchises?

c. Creator of a gaming style that emphasised learning and invention, the US designer Will Wright developed which 1989 game that let players build their own virtual urban worlds?

12 Derived from Russian, 'gulliver', meaning 'head', and 'horrorshow', meaning 'good', are slang words appearing in which British novel of 1962?

Three bonus questions on mythology

a. Which work by Ovid includes the story of the Ethiopian princess Andromeda, who is at risk of being sacrificed to a monster from the deep?

b. Andromeda was rescued by which son of Zeus and Danaë, renowned for slaying the Gorgon Medusa?

c. A story often confused with that of Perseus and Andromeda due to several similarities of plot, Ruggiero's saving of Angelica appears in which epic poem of 1516 by Ludovico Ariosto?

13 In palaeontology, a taxon that, as the result of a misidentification, appears to vanish from the fossil record and then reappear, is known informally by the name of which singer, in reference to the number of impersonators he has spawned?

Three bonus questions on a French composer

a. Which Frenchman became the first high-profile composer to write music for the cinema when he produced the score for the 1908 short film *The Assassination of the Duke of Guise*?

b. Featuring in the 1995 film *Babe*, the song 'If I Had Words' takes its melody from which work by Saint-Saëns?

c. The 'Aquarium' movement from which humorous musical suite by Saint-Saëns featured in Terrence Malick's 1978 film *Days of Heaven*?

14 The steeple of the Evangelical Reformed Church in Suurhusen and the spire of the Oberkirche in Bad Frankenhausen, both in Germany, share what form of aberration with the Campanile of Santa Maria Assunta in Pisa?

Three bonus questions on religion in AD 373

a. St Ephrem, who died in 373, was a noted writer of hymns and treatises in which liturgical language, a variety of Middle Aramaic?

b. A prominent opponent of Arianism, which Bishop of Alexandria died in 373? He gives his name to a creed that focuses on the doctrine of the Trinity.

c. Around 373, which saint founded the abbey of Marmoutier just outside the present-day city of Tours? There is a church dedicated to him on Trafalgar Square.

15 What type of object is being described if an example with a mass of 6.7 times 10 to the power 20 kilogrammes would have a radius of one-thousandth of a millimetre?

Three bonus questions on astronomy

a. Named after a German astronomer born in 1854, Kreutz Sungrazers are a related group of what astronomical objects?

b. The source of the Taurid meteor showers, and with an orbital period of only around three years, which comet was the second, after Halley's, to be shown to be periodic?

c. In what year is Halley's comet predicted to return to perihelion, or its closest approach to the Sun? You may have five years either side.

16 Give the chemical symbol that comes next in this sequence: N, O, F, Ne, and – what?

Three bonus questions on chemicals named after places. In each case, give the common name of the following.

a. Magnesium sulphate heptahydrate, named after a town in Surrey?

b. Potassium sodium tartrate tetrahydrate, named after a French seaport on the Bay of Biscay?

c. Calcium sulphate dihydrate, named after a European capital?

17 Listen carefully. Given two copies of the tesseract or four-dimensional hypercube, one with side-length twice that of the other, in what ratio are their volumes?

Three bonus questions on the sciences

a. Given the symbol CZ, what two-word term denotes an artificial diamond simulant, ultimately derived from a group four element used as a structural material in nuclear reactors?

b. The SI unit of volume, the cubic metre, is equivalent to how many litres?

c. In crystallography, 'cubic' is an alternative name for what system, in which the three axes are equal and mutually at right angles?

18 After an area now in South London, what two-word term is used of the discussions of 1647 between the council of the New Model Army and their commanders? They included radical political proposals, such as the argument for manhood suffrage.

Three bonus questions on the odes of John Keats

a. Which of Keats' odes ends with the lines 'Beauty is truth, truth beauty, – that is all / Ye know on earth, and all ye need to know'?

b. 'O latest-born and loveliest vision far / Of all Olympus' faded hierarchy!' Which goddess does Keats address with these words?

c. To what personification does Keats address the ode in which he asks 'Where are the songs of spring? Ay, where are they? / Think not of them, thou hast thy music too'?

19 In US politics, what two-word term denotes the body of 538 elected representatives who select the president and vice president?

Three bonus questions on pain

a. Meaning 'nerve pain', what medical term is used of pain in the area covered by a peripheral sensory nerve?

b. The term myalgia specifically refers to pain in what structures of the body?

c. Deriving from the Greek, the term rachialgia denotes pain in which part of the skeleton?

20 First used in an essay of 1849 by Henry David Thoreau, which two-word term describes the intentional, non-violent defiance of government authority on the grounds of moral objection, with the aim of promoting a just society?

Three bonus questions on a historical figure

a. Of the queens consort of England since 1066, who is the only one to have married four times? Her royal wedding, at Hampton Court in 1543, was the third of them.

b. Catherine Parr's second marriage, in 1534, was to which peer, a member of the same family as Warwick the Kingmaker of the previous century?

c. Catherine Parr's fourth and final marriage, in 1547, the same year that Henry VIII died, was to Thomas, the brother of which of Henry's other wives?

21 The advertising executive Maxwell Dane, the *Los Angeles Times* managing editor Ed Guthman and the actor Paul Newman were among the twenty names that comprised which US president's first 'Enemies List'?

Three bonus questions on a US president

a. In September 1974, which US president granted Richard Nixon a full and unconditional pardon, just before he could be indicted?

b. Pardoned by President Ford in 1977, Iva Toguri d'Aquino had been convicted of treason for broadcasting Japanese propaganda during the Second World War. By what two-word term were she and similar broadcasters better known?

c. Which Confederate commander in the Civil War signed an amnesty oath in 1865 but did not have his citizenship restored until 1975, by President Ford?

22 According to Faraday's First Law, the amount of a substance produced during electrolysis is proportional to what?

Three bonus questions on hypotheses

a. After a character in *Through the Looking Glass*, what name is given to the hypothesis that evolution will always continue in a given species in order to catch up with evolutionary advances made by competing species?

b. In economics, what two-word term denotes the hypothesis that an individual cannot make an abnormally high profit by trading on a financial market using widely available and generally understood information, as the market price will itself be influenced by the same information?

c. Named after a Greek goddess, which hypothesis was propounded by James Lovelock, and views the Earth as a self-sustaining living organism?

23 At the crossing point of the Trans-Siberian Railway and the River Ob, what is the largest city of Siberia and the third-largest of the Russian Republic?

Three bonus questions on place names

a. Bordering the remains of the Aral Sea, Karakalpakstan is the westernmost region of which former Soviet state?

b. Its name meaning 'mountain country', what is the southernmost federal subject of the Russian Republic? It is to the east of Chechnya, and has a coastline on the Caspian Sea.

c. A little smaller than Germany, and including much of the Thar Desert, what is the largest state of the Republic of India? Its capital is Jaipur.

24 What common five-letter word links: the oldest national park in the USA; the symbol of the Peak District National Park in the UK; an artefact deciphered by Jean-François Champollion; and the object that appears in the title of the first Harry Potter novel?

Three bonus questions on national parks in England

a. In which national park are Gaping Ghyll Cave, Mossdale Caverns, and the limestone ravine known as Gordale Scar?

b. The Lymington and Beaulieu rivers flow through which national park?

c. Dunkery Beacon is the highest point in which national park?

25 'One: You cannot win. Two: You cannot break even. Three: You cannot get out of the game.' These words, variously attributed to C.P. Snow and Isaac Asimov, sum up which physical principles governing the relationship between different forms of energy?

Three bonus questions on computer science

a. What low-level programming languages provide a symbolic representation of machine code particular to a specific computer architecture?

b. Including Fortran, Basic and 'C', what class of languages describe step-by-step the routines to be followed to achieve a desired program state?

c. What specific kind of languages may include features such as polymorphism, inheritance and messaging? Examples include 'C++', 'Java' and 'Python'?

26 Home to fifty-four cities, which island is described as being 'in the middle just 200 miles broad' and having a 'figure not unlike a crescent' in a work of 1516 by Thomas More?

Three bonus questions on indigenous peoples

a. Associated with regions such as Araucanía, the Mapuche are an indigenous people principally concentrated in which South American country?

b. Meaning 'of earliest times' and 'inhabitant', 'Adivasi' is an umbrella term for the indigenous peoples of which large Asian country?

   c. 'Orang Asli' is a collective term for the indigenous peoples of which country?

27 *First as Tragedy, then as Farce, The Sublime Object of Ideology* and *Living in the End Times* are among the works of which Marxist and cultural theorist, born in Ljubljana in 1949?

Three bonus questions on architecture

   a. Which Swiss architectural firm designed the 'Bird's Nest' stadium for the 2008 Olympic Games?

   b. Opened in 1992, the Goetz art gallery, also designed by Herzog and De Meuron, is in which European city?

   c. Which building, originally designed by Sir Giles Gilbert Scott, was renovated by Herzog and De Meuron in the mid-1990s to house the Tate Modern?

28 What term denotes artworks such as *The Garden of Earthly Delights* by Bosch, *The Merode Altarpiece* by Campin and *The Elevation of the Cross* by Rubens, all of which consist of a central panel with two hinged wings?

Three bonus questions on a Renaissance artist

   a. Much reproduced on greetings cards and T-shirts, the image of two cherubs, apparently leaning on the base of the painting and gazing at the figures above, is a detail of the *Sistine Madonna* by which Renaissance artist?

   b. The School of Athens was one of the frescoes painted by Raphael for which pope's private apartments in the Vatican?

   c. The painting generally believed to be Raphael's last before his early death in 1520 depicts, and takes its title from, which event in the life of Jesus? It took place on a mountaintop in the presence of Peter, James and John.

29 What surname is shared by the thirteenth-century philosopher and scientist also known as Dr Mirabilis, a philosopher and statesman knighted by James I, and the Dublin-born artist who painted the 1945 *Three Figures at the Base of the Crucifixion*?

Three bonus questions on 'third men'

a. The 'third man' argument is an examination of the theory of forms in the dialogue *Parmenides*, written by which philosopher?

b. The 'third man' syndrome, in which explorers imagine or hallucinate the presence of one more member of their team than is actually present, is described in *South*, an account by which explorer of his Antarctic expedition of 1914 to 1917?

c. Who is the author of the 2010 memoir *The Third Man*, which the *Independent* newspaper recommended to 'anyone remotely interested in politics, psychiatry and theatre'?

30 During the 1980s, which Cabinet position was held by Lord Carrington, Francis Pym, Geoffrey Howe, John Major and Douglas Hurd?

Three bonus questions on foreign secretaries, in the words of the Foreign and Commonwealth Office website. Identify the minister from the description. All three served before 1968.

a. 'A former Prime Minister, he cultivated a fine taste for good food, lawn tennis and philosophy. At the Paris peace conference, his behaviour was likened to that of a choir boy at a funeral service.'

b. 'His subordinates found him unusually modest.
He nevertheless became the first British Foreign
Secretary to win the Nobel Peace Prize, following his ...
negotiation of the Treaty of Locarno in 1925.'

c. 'At the important Anglo-German meeting at
Berchtesgaden in 1938, he mistook Hitler for
a doorman.'

> 'Somehow *University Challenge*
> has managed to avoid its
> questions being trivia questions.
> They come from a place that
> is more related, still, to the idea of
> learning, and that's a very
> good thing.'
>
> STEPHEN FRY
> (actor, writer)
> Contestant, 1980

The Answers

1. -ob (if they buzz in with specific word, press for the final two letters; nabob, carob, shelob)
   a. Charles Darwin
   b. Lazarus
   c. William Shakespeare

2. Gallstones (accept calculi)
   a. (Rat) flea / *Xenopsylla cheopsis* (aka Oriental rat flea, tropical rat flea)
   b. Ticks / *Ixodes* species
   c. Tsetse fly / *Glossina* species

3. Bed (Brownell, Edward, Davison)
   a. Minim
   b. Pip
   c. Malayalam

4. Quadrat (not quadrant)
   a. Stigma, style and ovary
   b. Ovary wall / outer layer of the ovary (if just 'ovary', prompt for the specific part)
   c. Nut

5. Ear / cochlea (i.e. the tapered cavity of the inner ear)
   a. Limb and limbo
   b. Prim and primo
   c. Gust and gusto

6 Holography
   a. Socratic and acrostic
   b. Gordian and adoring
   c. Arbiter and rarebit

7 (John) Milton (Satan, in *Paradise Lost*, Book 1, 254)
   a. Graham Greene
   b. W.H. Auden
   c. (Ernest) Hemingway ('It's due tomorrow. I totally have to hemingway that term paper tonight.')

8 (Hanyu) Pinyin
   a. (C. Auguste) Dupin – (Edgar Allan) Poe (the OED's first citation of 'detective' is 1843)
   b. (Jules) Maigret – (Georges) Simenon
   c. (Jacques) Clouseau – Blake Edwards (with Maurice Richlin)

9 Factotum (Latin: *fac*, imp. of *facere*, 'do'; *totum*, 'everything'. 'Largo al factotum della citta')
   a. (Sir) Stanley Matthews
   b. 50 (so accept 49, 50, 51)
   c. Blackpool

10 Vorticists (the manifesto in *Blast*)
   a. Nihilism
   b. Fyodor Dostoyevsky
   c. Oscar Wilde

11 Beach (*Einstein on the Beach*, 'Dover Beach', *On Chesil Beach*)
   a. Sid Meier (a 'god game' enables a player to control a game on a large scale)
   b. (Shigeru) Miyamoto
   c. *Simcity* (not *Simlife*, which was later, in 1992; not *The Sims*, which was later still, in 2000)

12 (A) *Clockwork Orange* (by Anthony Burgess, of course; Russian: *golova*, 'head'; *khorosho*, 'good')

    a. *Metamorphoses*
    b. Perseus
    c. *Orlando Furioso*

13 Elvis (taxon)

    a. (Camille) Saint-Saëns
    b. Third symphony (or Organ Symphony in C Minor)
    c. *Carnival of the Animals*

14 They lean / leaning

    a. Syriac
    b. St Athanasius
    c. St Martin (of Tours)

15 A black hole (i.e. a micrometre = one-thousandth of a millimetre)

    a. Comets (because their orbits are very close to the Sun at perihelion, and formed from the remnants of one large comet; Heinrich Kreutz, 1854–1907)
    b. Encke (designated 2P/Encke; named after Johann Franz Encke, 1791–1865, who calculated its orbit)
    c. 2061 (so accept 2056 to 2066)

16 Na (elements 7–10; sodium is 11)

    a. Epsom salt (accept epsomite)
    b. Rochelle salt
    c. Plaster of Paris

17 16 to 1 (accept: 1 to 16, 16, 1/16)

    a. Cubic zirconia (accept cubic zirconium / cubic zircona; not zircon, zirconium)
    b. One thousand
    c. Isometric (system)

18 Putney Debates

     a. 'Ode on a Grecian Urn'
     b. Psyche ('Ode to Psyche')
     c. Autumn ('Ode to Autumn')

19 Electoral college
     a. Neuralgia
     b. Muscles
     c. Spine (Greek: *rhakis*, 'spine')

20 Civil disobedience ('On the Duty of Civil Disobedience')
     a. Catherine Parr
     b. (John) Neville / Baron Latimer (either name is acceptable)
     c. Jane Seymour

21 (Richard M.) Nixon (Dane produced pro-Democrat advertising; Guthman had been Robert Kennedy's press secretary; Newman opposed the Vietnam War)
     a. Gerald Ford
     b. Tokyo Rose
     c. Robert E. Lee

22 Quantity of electricity / (electrical) charge transferred / charge passed (not 'electrical current')
     a. Red Queen (Hypothesis)
     b. Efficient Market(s) (Hypothesis)
     c. Gaia (Hypothesis)

23 Novosibirsk
     a. Uzbekistan
     b. Dagestan
     c. Rajasthan

24 Stone (Yellowstone, millstone, Rosetta Stone, Philosopher's Stone)
     a. Yorkshire Dales
     b. New Forest
     c. Exmoor

25 (Laws of) Thermodynamics
- **a.** Assembly languages / codes (accept assembler)
- **b.** Procedural languages / imperative languages
- **c.** Object-oriented languages

26 Utopia
- **a.** Chile (a much smaller population, around 18 per cent that of Chile, is found in Argentina)
- **b.** India
- **c.** Malaysia

27 Slavoj Zizek
- **a.** Herzog & De Meuron
- **b.** Munich
- **c.** Bankside Power Station

28 Triptych
- **a.** Raphael
- **b.** Julius II (Raphael also worked for his successor, Leo X, after Julius's death in 1513)
- **c.** Transfiguration (not 'Ascension', of course)

29 Bacon (Roger Bacon and two Francis Bacons)
- **a.** Plato
- **b.** (Ernest) Shackleton
- **c.** Peter Mandelson (subtitled *Life at the Heart of New Labour*)

30 Foreign Secretary
- **a.** (Arthur) Balfour (served 1916–1919)
- **b.** (Austen) Chamberlain (served 1924–1929)
- **c.** (Viscount) Halifax (served 1938–1940)

Match Ten

1 Which West Indian cricketer and High Commissioner of Trinidad and Tobago was created Baron of Maraval and Nelson in 1969, and subsequently became the first person of African extraction to take a seat in the House of Lords?

Three bonus questions on cricket

a. Jack Hobbs in 1923, Len Hutton in 1951 and Viv Richards in 1988 are among the small number of batsmen who have achieved what cricketing milestone?

b. Which batsman was the first to make his hundredth hundred in the twenty-first century, for Surrey against Yorkshire in 2008?

c. Which Yorkshire batsman was the first to make his hundredth hundred in a Test match, for England against Australia at Headingley in 1977?

2 In one of the first attempts at climate classification, the ancient Greeks divided the Earth into three zones: torrid, temperate and which other, referring to the 'uninhabitable' areas in the far north and far south?

Three bonus questions on climatology

a. Resulting from an expedition to St Helena, which English astronomer and meteorologist produced a chart in 1686 that documented trade winds and monsoons, and identified solar heating as the cause of atmospheric motions?

b. Which Serbian astrophysicist, who died in 1958, dedicated his career to developing a mathematical theory of climate based on the seasonal and latitudinal variations of solar radiation received by the Earth?

c. Of German descent, which climatologist in 1900 classified climatic types by relating them to the Earth's natural vegetation zones, and later defined them in terms of mean annual temperature and precipitation?

3 In North America, a rich tart consisting of treacle baked in a pastry case has what name, referring to the need to wave insects away from the filling?

Three bonus questions on football

a. In 1889, which Lancashire club became the first Football League champions? The club were champions in the next season and runners-up in the next three seasons.

b. In 1926, which Yorkshire club became the first to win the English First Division championship three times in succession?

c. What was the next club to win the League championship in three successive years? I want the name of the club and the decade in which they achieved the feat.

4 Which character in Shakespeare's *A Midsummer Night's Dream* shares his name with a fruit? The latter has a tough flesh and yellow skin, and the former is a carpenter and producer of amateur dramatics who performs the prologue in the play-within-the-play?

Three bonus questions on novels whose titles are taken from plays by Shakespeare

a. *Cakes and Ale*, taken from a line in *Twelfth Night*, is a novel of 1930 by which author?

b. Which novel of 1872 by Thomas Hardy takes its title from the first line of a song performed by Amiens in *As You Like It*?

c. Forming the title of a 1968 novel by Agatha Christie, which six words precede the line: 'Something wicked this way comes', spoken by one of the witches in *Macbeth*?

5 Used as an expression to denote an outcast, what name is given in the Book of Genesis to the son of Abraham by his wife's maidservant Hagar, and was given by Melville to the narrator of Moby-Dick?

Three bonus questions on former Soviet republics, from the opening sentence of the country's introduction in the CIA *World Factbook*. In each case, identify the country from the description.

a. '[This country's] lands were united under Mindaugas in 1236; over the next century, through alliances and conquest, [it] extended its territory to include most of present-day Belarus and Ukraine'?

b. 'For centuries [the eastern part of this country] formed part of the Persian province of Khurasan; in medieval times Merv was one of the great cities of the Islamic world'?

c. 'Formerly part of Romania [this country] was incorporated into the Soviet Union at the close of World War Two'?

6 'Out of the mountain of despair, a stone of hope.' These words form one of the inscriptions on a memorial in Washington DC to which campaigner, assassinated in Memphis, Tennessee in April 1968?

Three bonus questions on the British actor Charles Laughton

a. Which Roman emperor did Charles Laughton play in Cecil B. DeMille's 1932 film *The Sign of the Cross*?

b. What role did Laughton play in the 1953 film *Salome*? He memorably views Rita Hayworth, in the title role, performing the Dance of the Seven Veils.

c. Laughton won the 1933 Academy Award for Best Actor for his role as which English king? He later played the same king in *Young Bess*.

7 Quote: 'I thought ten thousand swords must have leaped from their scabbards to avenge even a look that threatened her with insult. But the age of chivalry is gone...' These words of Edmund Burke refer to which royal figure, executed in 1793?

Three bonus questions on US universities. In each case, I want the city and state in which the following are based.

a. Johns Hopkins University, founded in 1876?

b. Duke University, founded in 1838?

c. Brown University, founded in 1764?

8 Born in 1858, which German physicist gives his name to a 'length' of around about 10 to the minus 20 of the diameter of a proton?

Three bonus questions on physics

a. A space station in a low Earth orbit of 300 kilometres altitude experiences what acceleration due to Earth's gravity? Give your answer in metres per second squared, to the nearest whole number.

b. In a circular orbit, the square of the orbital speed is equal to acceleration multiplied by what quantity?

c. Therefore, with an orbital radius of approximately 6,700 kilometres, what is the space station's speed in kilometres per second, to the nearest whole number?

9 Its themes including the commercialisation of Christmas, the 2007 documentary film *What Would Jesus Buy?* was produced by which US filmmaker, whose works include *Failure Club* and *Super Size Me?*

Three bonus questions on history. In each case, give the century before the Christian Era in which the following took place.

a. The reign of King Ashoka in India; the making of the Terracotta Army in China; and Hannibal's crossing of the Alps?

b. The death of Zoroaster; the birth of Confucius; and the founding of the Roman Republic?

c. Finally, the destruction of Nineveh by the Medes and Babylonians; and the establishment of Draco's code of laws in Athens?

10 What precise year saw the reversal of Puritan legislation of the 1640s that had banned celebrations at Christmas?

Three bonus questions on modern Irish theatre

a. First seen in 1996, which play for two actors by Marie Jones is about the filming of a Hollywood movie in the County Kerry countryside, as seen through the eyes of two local extras?

b. *Shining City* and *The Seafarer* are plays by which Dublin-born playwright? He won the 1999 Olivier Award for best new play with *The Weir*.

c. Which London-born Irish dramatist, the director of the film *In Bruges*, staged his first play, *The Beauty Queen of Leenane*, on Broadway in 1998?

11 Spell the six-letter name of the building designed by the Richard Rogers Partnership that opened on St David's Day 2006 to house the Welsh Assembly?

Three bonus questions on South American presidents

a. Named after the man who took office in 1956 and was later forced into exile by the military junta, Presidente Juscelino Kubitschek International Airport serves which city?

b. Which once-exiled professor of sociology became in 1998 the first Brazilian president to be re-elected for a second four-year term?

c. His successor, a former shoe-shine boy and founding member of the Workers' Party, is known by what short nickname?

12 Listen carefully and answer as soon as your name is called. If the twenty-four days of an Advent calendar are randomly assigned twenty-four different pictures, six of which contain a reindeer, what is the probability of revealing a reindeer on Christmas Eve?

Three bonus questions on mathematics

a. In mathematics, what name denotes the infinite set of real numbers that are not algebraic, meaning that they are not the solution of any polynomial equation with integer coefficients?

b. E, or Napier's Constant, was first proved to be transcendental in a paper of 1873 by which French mathematician?

c. The first proof that pi is transcendental was provided in the 1880s by the German mathematician Ferdinand von Lindemann, and immediately implied that which of the so-called 'geometric problems of antiquity' is insoluble?

13 Listen carefully. Father Christmas and his sleigh can travel the 40,000 kilometres around the globe in 12 hours. To the nearest day, how long would it take him to fly non-stop the 400,000 kilometres to the Moon?

Three bonus questions on the Solar System

a. Which planet of the Solar System has the shortest rotational period, of 9 hours 55 minutes?

b. Which planet's orbital period is closest to the average human life expectancy in the developed world?

c. Which planet orbits the Sun roughly a thousand times during one complete orbit of Pluto?

14 'Easter', 'Thanksgiving' and 'Christmas' are closely related varieties of which plant? *Schlumbergera x buckleyi* is the Christmas variety, a popular houseplant with flattened, jointed stems which is grown for its cerise flowers that appear around this time of year?

Three bonus questions on a battle

a. Roncesvalles, a pass in the Pyrenees, is traditionally regarded as the site of the defeat by Basque forces of the army of which king of the Franks in 778?

b. What is the name of the nephew of Charlemagne who was killed at Roncesvalles and who is immortalised in an eleventh-century chanson, or song?

c. 'The Song of Roland' is a major theme in the 1939 novel *The Confidential Agent* by which British author?

15 Give your answer either in square metres or square feet. According to the Christmas Day (Trading) Act of 2004, shops in England and Wales over what internal floor area are not allowed to open on Christmas Day?

Three bonus questions on a royal palace

a. In Jerome K. Jerome's *Three Men in a Boat*, Harris proposes a visit to a tourist attraction with these ill-founded words: 'We'll just walk round for ten minutes, then go and get some lunch.' To which attraction, at which royal palace, was he referring?

b. In the Lower Orangery of Hampton Court, *The Triumphs of Caesar* is a set of nine canvasses by which Italian artist, a court painter to Ludovico Gonzaga of Mantua?

c. Which cardinal gives his name to a closet in the palace that carries his motto: *Dominus mihi adjutor*, 'The Lord is my helper'?

16 Quote: 'A noble dish is a turkey, roast or boiled. A Christmas dinner with the middle classes of this Empire, would scarcely be a Christmas dinner without its turkey.' Who wrote these words, in her book of household management, published in book form in 1861?

Three bonus questions on a building in Rome

a. Having the largest unreinforced concrete dome in the world, the Church of Santa Maria Rotonda is also known by what single-word name?

b. The only source of natural light in the Pantheon is a round opening in the centre of the dome around 8 metres in diameter and known by what Latin name, indicating an organ of the body?

c. In the seventeenth century, the Pantheon's roof was stripped of bronze for use in which artist's altar canopy in St Peter's?

17 Introduced by the US sociologists George Kelling and James Wilson in 1982, which sociological theory holds that the vandalism of a few eponymous building features can quickly lead to more destruction and further local crime?

Three bonus questions on world history

a. Which decade of the twentieth century links the Long March of the Chinese Communists, the 'Chaco War' between Bolivia and Paraguay, and the establishment of Saudi Arabia?

b. Which decade of the nineteenth century saw the end of convict transportation to Australia, the emancipation of the serfs in Russia, and the unification of Italy?

c. Which decade of the eighteenth century saw James Cook claim what is now New South Wales for Britain, and Bostonians throw tea into the harbour in a protest over tax?

18 'The woman every woman wished was her best friend.' These words refer to which US screenwriter, who died in 2012? Her comedies include *You've Got Mail* and *When Harry Met Sally*.

Three bonus questions on satire

a. 'It is difficult not to write satire.' These are the words of which poet, who was banished to Egypt after writing sixteen satires that exposed the immorality of Roman society?

b. 'Satire is a lesson,' wrote Vladimir Nabokov. What similar genre of writing did he describe as 'a game'?

c. 'Satire, being levelled at all, is never resented for an offence by any.' Who wrote these words in the preface to his 1704 work *A Tale of a Tub*?

19 *The Human Condition, The Pleasure Principle* and *The Treachery of Images* are paintings by which surrealist? A museum in Brussels is dedicated to his work.

Three bonus questions on place names in England. In each case, your answer will be two towns or cities whose names share a common suffix, 'London' and 'Swindon', for example.

a. A town in North Derbyshire perhaps best known for the shape of its church's spire, and a West Yorkshire town noted for its Victorian architecture and for having an unusually large number of listed buildings?

b. A port on the River Medway, site of a former Royal Navy dockyard, and the metropolitan borough immediately north-east of Manchester, birthplace of the composer William Walton?

c. The cathedral city closest to Stonehenge, and a county town on the River Severn, the birthplace of Charles Darwin?

20 Answer as soon as your name is called. Which two prime numbers, when multiplied together, give the total number of kilometres in the two events in which Mo Farah won Gold in the 2012 Olympics?

Three bonus questions on chemical elements

a. A figure of Greek mythology who served his own son Pelops as a dish in a banquet for the gods is the source of the name of which transition metal, used in the manufacture of surgical instruments and mobile phone capacitors.

b. Which element is found in the ore tantalite, and is named after the daughter of Tantalus?

c. The element titanium is named after the mythological Titans; which element takes its name from the individual Titan who was the son of Iapetus?

21 'She came to prove Solomon with hard questions at Jerusalem, with ... camels that bare spices, and gold in abundance.' These words from the Book of Chronicles refer to which ruler? She gives her name to a sinfonia by Handel often played at weddings.

Three bonus questions on transport

a. In which island group are Westray and Papa Westray, which are connected by what is claimed to be the world's shortest scheduled flight, lasting around two minutes?

b. Which Kentish port is the most easterly town in Britain that is directly connected to the motorway system?

c. What is the most northerly town in Britain to be directly connected to the national rail network?

22 In addition to the Precambrian and the Cambrian, two geological periods have names associated with Wales. Name either of them.

Three bonus questions on mineralogy

a. What name is commonly given to the crystalline form of aluminium oxide, Al_2O_3?

b. What name is given to the group of crystalline aluminium silicate minerals which collectively are the most abundant minerals in the crust of the Earth?

c. What is the chemical formula for quartz, the second most common mineral in the Earth's crust?

23 Give both answers promptly after your name is called. Meaning 'hearty, warm and friendly', and 'squeeze or crush', what two words, by an extension of their respective etymologies, both denote a sweet, non-alcoholic syrup used as the basis of a soft drink or as a mixer in a cocktail?

Three bonus questions on words coined in the twentieth century. In each case, give the decade in which the following originated, according to the Oxford English Dictionary.

a. First, for five points: cubism, allergy, isotope and profiteer?

b. Second: disinformation, hallucinogenic, meritocracy and modem?

c. Finally: biodiversity, liposuction, wannabe and shopaholic?

24 Listen carefully. Which two words are anagrams of each other, and mean the plural of the SI unit of electrical resistance, and the scale of mineral hardness named after a German geologist?

Three bonus questions on electromagnetic radiation

a. What three-letter acronym denotes the spectroscopy in which radio-frequency radiation flips nuclear spins within a sample placed in a magnetic field?

b. Which German physicist gives his name to a form of spectroscopy involving the measurement of the absorption of gamma radiation by nuclei?

c. Born in 1845, which German scientist discovered X-rays?

25 In animal behaviour, what general term denotes a form of learning that is rapid, irreversible, and occurs during a short critical period in early life? It was first described in detail by Konrad Lorenz, in connection with the goslings of greylag geese.

Three bonus questions on immunology

a. Immunoglobulin proteins have roughly Y-shaped molecules composed of heavy and light chains. What are the two external domains or regions to which antigens bind?

b. What is the tip of the fab region called? It recognises and binds to specific antigens.

c. To which region of an antigen does the paratope of an immunoglobulin bind?

26 Haversian canals are found in which tissue of the body? They contain small vessels responsible for the blood supply to osteocytes.

Three bonus questions on bone morphology

a. The frontal, coronal, sagittal and squamosal are among the fibrous tissues that ossify gradually after birth to fuse the plate-like bones forming which specific structure of the human skeleton?

b. Articulating with the lumbar vertebra above and the coccyx below, which wedge-shaped bone of the adult human body is made up mainly of five vertebrae which are separate in childhood, and become fully fused only by about the 26th year?

c. Developed in the tendon of the quadriceps femoris, which bone of the leg ossifies usually from a single nucleus of cartilaginous tissue at around the age of 3 to 6?

27 What common name is given to insects of the order Dermaptera? They are distinguished by membranous wings folded under short forewings, and by pincer-like sensory appendages on the abdomen.

Three bonus questions on microbiology

a. In terms of reproduction, what characterises the Deuteromycota, also known as *Fungi imperfecti*?

b. Mucor is known as 'pin mould' because of the appearance of the structures in which asexual spores are formed. What are these structures called?

c. What is the common name of unicellular members of the phylum Ascomycotina that reproduce by budding rather than by spore formation?

28 What pervasive presence did the veteran *New York Times* journalist Murray Schumach describe as 'the bland leading the bland'?

Three bonus questions on a Greek island

a. According to Herodotus, which Aegean island was notable for its Temple of Hera and the Tunnel of Eupalinos, an early aqueduct? Both now form part of a UNESCO World Heritage Site.

b. A native of Samos, which third-century astronomer anticipated Copernicus by asserting that the Earth moves around the Sun?

c. Born in Samos around 570 BC, which scientist and mystic founded a religious colony in south Italy, and is credited with a large number of mathematical discoveries?

29 Inserting the word 'ones', after the third letter transforms the English name of one Asian country into that of another. For ten points, name both.

Three bonus questions on literary advice

a. Give the sense of the idea that completes this sentence in Boswell's *Life of Dr Johnson*: 'Read over your compositions, and where ever you meet with a passage which you think particularly fine ...'?

b. His achievements including the 1900 version of *The Oxford Book of English Verse*, which critic advised his readers to 'murder your darlings ... whenever you feel an impulse to perpetrate a piece of exceptionally fine writing'?

c. The phrase 'kill your darlings' is most often attributed to which US Nobel laureate, the author of *Light in August* and *As I Lay Dying*?

30 *Euclid and his Modern Rivals*, published in 1879, and a paper on Zeno's paradoxes entitled 'What the Tortoise Said to Achilles' are works by which literary figure, better known for his books for children?

Three bonus questions on paradoxes

a. The paradox of self-reference, or the liar paradox, is expressed in what statement attributed to Epimenides the Cretan? It is usually expressed in four words.

b. Named after a British logician, Jourdain's paradox has a two-sided card. On one side are the words 'The statement on the other side of this card is false'; what is written on the other side?

c. What two-word term indicates a situation in which a statement is shown to entail its negation and vice versa? It is also commonly used of a condition in which an action and reaction intensify each other, with unfavourable results.

The Answers

1 Learie (Nicholas) Constantine (1901–1971)
   a. A hundred hundreds / 100 (first-class) centuries
   b. (Mark) Ramprakash (Graeme Hick's 100th was in 1998)
   c. (Geoffrey) Boycott

2 Frigid (zone)
   a. (Edmond) Halley
   b. (Milutin) Milankovitch (now known as the Milankovitch theory)
   c. (Wladimir) Köppen

3 Shoo-fly pie
   a. Preston (North End)
   b. Huddersfield (Town)
   c. Arsenal, 1930s (1933–1935)

4 (Peter) Quince
   a. (William) Somerset Maugham
   b. *Under the Greenwood Tree*
   c. 'By the pricking of my thumbs'

5 Ishmael
   a. Lithuania
   b. Turkmenistan
   c. Moldova (not Moldavia, which is a historical region not a present-day country)

6 Martin Luther King

a. Nero
b. (King) Herod
c. Henry VIII (*The Private Life of Henry VIII*)

7 Marie Antoinette (*Reflections on the Revolution in France*)
  a. Baltimore, Maryland
  b. Durham, North Carolina
  c. Providence, Rhode Island

8 (Max) Planck
  a. 9 (radius of Earth 6,360 km, so gravity is 6,360/6m660=0.955 times g or 9.8*0.955=9.35m/s2)
  b. (Orbital) radius
  c. 8

9 Morgan Spurlock
  a. Third (300–201 BCE)
  b. Sixth (600–501 BCE)
  c. Seventh (700–601 BCE)

10 1660
  a. *Stones in His Pockets*
  b. Conor McPherson
  c. Martin McDonagh

11 S-e-n-e-d-d (it stands in Cardiff Bay)
  a. Brasilia
  b. (Fernando Henrique) Cardoso
  c. Lula (Luiz Inácio Lula da Silva)

12 One in four / 0.25
  a. Transcendental (numbers)
  b. (Charles) Hermite (1822–1901)
  c. Squaring the circle / quadrature of the circle (i.e., using a compass and straightedge in finite steps, to construct a square with the same area as a given circle)

13 Five days (he can travel 80,000km a day, so 400,000 / 80,000 = 5 days)

- **a.** Jupiter
- **b.** Uranus (around 84 Earth years; Saturn just under 30 years; Neptune just under 165)
- **c.** Mercury (about 1,030 times)

14 Cactus / zygocactus

- **a.** Charlemagne / Charles the Great
- **b.** Roland
- **c.** Graham Greene

15 280 square metres / 3,000 square feet

- **a.** The maze at Hampton Court
- **b.** (Andrea) Mantegna
- **c.** (Cardinal Thomas) Wolsey

16 Mrs (Isabella) Beeton

- **a.** Pantheon
- **b.** Oculus
- **c.** (Gian Lorenzo) Bernini

17 Broken windows theory

- **a.** 1930s (1934–1935; 1932–1935; 1932)
- **b.** 1860s (1868, 1861, 1861)
- **c.** 1770s (1770, 1773)

18 Nora Ephron

- **a.** Juvenal
- **b.** Parody
- **c.** (Jonathan) Swift

19 (René) Magritte

- **a.** Chesterfield and Huddersfield
- **b.** Chatham and Oldham
- **c.** Salisbury and Shrewsbury

20 3 and 5 (5,000 and 10,000 metres of course)
  a. Tantalum (after Tantalus)
  b. Niobium (after Niobe)
  c. Promethium (after Prometheus)

21 Queen of Sheba
  a. Orkney / Orkney Islands
  b. Folkestone
  c. Thurso

22 Ordovician / Silurian
  a. Corundum
  b. Feldspars
  c. SiO_2

23 Cordial and squash
  a. 1910s
  b. 1950s
  c. 1980s

24 Ohms and mohs (Friedrich Mohs, 1773–1839)
  a. N.M.R. (i.e. Nuclear Magnetic Resonance [spectroscopy]; accept P.M.R., proton magnetic resonance [spectroscopy])
  b. (Rudolf Ludwig) Mössbauer (1929–2011; recoilless nuclear resonance fluorescence)
  c. (Wilhelm Conrad) Röntgen (1845–1923)

25 (Filial) imprinting
  a. Fab or fab fragment(s) / fragment antigen binding (region)
  b. Paratope
  c. Epitope

26 (Compact) bone
  a. The cranium (not skull, which includes both cranium

and mandible)
- **b.** The sacrum
- **c.** The patella or kneecap

27 Earwigs
- **a.** Lack a sexual stage / reproduce only asexually (i.e. produces either no spores or asexual spores)
- **b.** Sporangia / sporangiospores
- **c.** Yeasts (i.e. the 'true yeasts', baker's yeast, candida)

28 Television
- **a.** Samos
- **b.** Aristarchus
- **c.** Pythagoras

29 India and Indonesia
- **a.** '... strike it out'
- **b.** (Sir Arthur) Quiller-Couch
- **c.** (William) Faulkner

30 Lewis Carroll (Charles Lutwidge Dodgson)
- **a.** All Cretans are liars
- **b.** 'The statement on the other side of this card is true'
- **c.** Vicious circle

Match Eleven

1 Which philosopher's conviction that only a select few are able to free themselves from ignorance and achieve true knowledge is exemplified by the Allegory of the Cave, described in a dialogue between Glaucon and Socrates?

Three bonus questions on the documentaries of Werner Herzog

a. The 2010 3D film *Cave of Forgotten Dreams* saw Herzog gain exclusive access to which cave in southern France, discovered in 1994?

b. The late environmentalist and bear activist Timothy Treadwell is the title subject of which 2005 documentary?

c. The 1999 documentary *My Best Fiend* (sic) concerns Herzog's relationship with which German actor, reputed to be somewhat 'difficult'? He played the title roles in Herzog's films *Fitzcarraldo* and *Nosferatu*.

2 As depicted in a series of paintings by Edouard Manet, which Austrian archduke and Emperor of Mexico was executed by firing squad in June 1867?

Three bonus questions on the legislative assemblies of EU member states. In each case, name the *city* in which the following parliament buildings are located.

a. First, for five points: the Binnenhof?

b. Second: Toompea Castle?

c. Finally: the Grandmaster's Palace?

3 Seven months and ten days is the shortest period of time to have elapsed between UK general elections in the twentieth century. In which year did this happen?

Three bonus questions on boroughs that had their parliamentary representation reduced by the Second Reform Act of 1867. In each case, name the place from the description.

a. A cathedral city on the River Ure in Yorkshire, close to Fountains Abbey?

b. The southernmost town of Lincolnshire, noted for an unusually large number of listed buildings?

c. A cathedral city in South Staffordshire? In 1709 it was the birthplace of Dr Johnson.

4 What short noun links 'Crow', 'Ghost' and 'Famished' in the titles of novels by Iain Banks, Pat Barker and Ben Okri?

Three bonus questions on novels

a. James Ellroy's *American Tabloid* and Don DeLillo's *Libra* are among novels that offer accounts of which event of November 1963?

b. 'The Assassination of John Fitzgerald Kennedy Considered as a Downhill Motor Race' is a story in *The Atrocity Exhibition*, an experimental collection by which British novelist, who died in 2009?

c. Combining the Kennedy assassination with the theme of time travel, *11/22/63* is a novel of 2011 by which popular US author?

5 Formerly subject to the Qing empire, when its name was preceded by the word 'Outer', which modern Asian state borders an autonomous region of northern China that shares its name, preceded by the word 'Inner'?

Three bonus questions on exclamation marks

a. The name of which village on Bideford Bay is taken from the title of a novel by Charles Kingsley, and is unusual amongst British place names in that it contains an exclamation mark?

b. Released in 1968, what was the first film with an exclamation mark in its title to win the Oscar for Best Picture?

c. In 1965, two UK number one songs had exclamation marks in their titles. 'Go Now!' by The Moody Blues was one. What was the other? I want the name of the song and the band.

6 Meaning 'beautiful form', what Greek-derived term denotes an optical instrument consisting of several reflecting surfaces in a tube, one end of which contains pieces of coloured glass?

Three bonus questions on words from the Greek. In each case, give the word from the definition. To make it a little easier, they all end with the same three letters.

  a. A tall jar or jug with two handles and a narrow neck?

  b. An excess or overabundance of something?

  c. A public open space, used for markets or assemblies?

7 Work this out before you buzz. If an ideal gas at zero degrees Celsius is heated steadily at constant pressure, at what temperature, to the nearest degree, will it occupy twice its original volume?

Three bonus questions on gases

  a. In joules per kelvin per mole, what is the numerical value, to the nearest integer, of the gas constant that appears in the ideal, or perfect, gas equation?

  b. What name is given to the ratio of the molar volume of a non-perfect gas to the molar volume of a perfect gas at the same pressure and temperature?

  c. Derived from the Latin for 'force', what name is given to the series of coefficients that appear in the generalised formulation of the perfect gas equation for non-perfect gases?

8 In the USA, for what do the letters 'HP' stand in the abbreviation NRHP, a national register of various sites and structures deemed worthy of preservation?

Three bonus questions on African countries and their coastlines, according to the CIA *World Factbook*

  a. Ahead of South Africa and Morocco, which country has the longest coastline of any on the African continent, more than 3,000 kilometres in length?

b. Of the countries of West Africa, two have coastlines of less than 100 kilometres. One is Gambia, which is the other?

c. The shortest coastline of any country in Africa is 37 kilometres long, on either side of the estuary of which major river, after which the country is named?

9 Listen carefully. The 2010 film comedy-drama *Tamara Drewe* is based on the graphic novel by Posy Simmonds which was itself based on which novel by Thomas Hardy?

Three bonus questions on the year 1565

a. Which major city of the southern hemisphere dates its first buildings to 1565? Its site had been named on 1 January 1502, by Portuguese sailors believing its bay to be a river mouth.

b. In 1565, Miguel López de Legazpi founded Cebu, the first permanent Spanish settlement in which present-day country?

c. St Augustine, the oldest remaining European settlement in the USA, was founded by Spain in 1565. In which state is it?

10 What two initials link the contemporary philosopher who wrote 'An Essay on Kindness'; the author of the lyrics of 'Land of Hope and Glory'; a US market analyst who gives his name to a system of television ratings, and the local rivals of Inter Milan?

Three bonus questions on the classification of galaxies

a. Most large galaxies fall into two broad morphological classes, known by the abbreviations 'S' and 'E'. For which two terms do these letters stand?

b. A satellite of the Andromeda spiral galaxy called Andromeda V is an example of what small, dim class of galaxy, abbreviated 'dSph'?

c. Galaxies are often classified by characteristics other than morphology. Those denoted by the acronym ULIRG, such as Arp 220, are characterised by luminosity. For what do the letters ULIRG stand?

11 What six-letter word can be preceded, in biology, by 'mitochondrial', in statistics, by 'decision', and in printing, by 'dot'?

Three bonus questions on bacteriology

a. Which widely used staining technique for the initial identification of bacteria, devised in 1884, is named after its Danish inventor?

b. In Gram staining, the bacteria are treated with a dye which is retained by the Gram-positive bacteria. What colour is this dye?

c. The bacteria are flushed with a chemical solution followed by an organic solvent. What is the main chemical in the initial flushing solution?

12 'The Drunkard's Holiday', 'Dr Diver's Holiday' and 'Richard Diver' were all working titles for which novel of 1934 by F. Scott Fitzgerald?

Three bonus questions on Spanish wine

a. According to a widely circulated remark, Sir Alexander Fleming said that 'if penicillin can cure those that are ill', which Spanish drink 'can bring the dead back to life'?

b. Sharing its name with an elevated plateau in the centre of the country, which Spanish wine region is usually said to be the world's largest continuous vine-growing region?

c. Which region's wineries are divided into the three districts of Alavesa, Alta and Baja?

13 The Latin phrase *indocilis privata loqui*, which translates as 'not apt to disclose secrets', is the motto of which organisation? It consists of both professional and amateur members, and was formed in London in 1905.

Three bonus questions on the measurement of the circle

a. Whose treatise of the third century BC was entitled *The Measurement of the Circle*, and includes the first rigorous calculation of pi?

b. 'I am ashamed to tell you to how many figures I carried these computations, having no other business at the time.' Which scientist wrote these words in a letter of 1666, having computed pi to 15 digits?

c. What are the first five digits of the binary expansion of pi?

14 Linguistically speaking, what links the place-names Pendle Hill, Isle of Sheppey and River Tyne?

Three bonus questions on pairs of place names. In each case, the letters in the first name form the first part of the second name – for example, the Belgian town 'Spa' and the country 'Spain'. Give both names from the descriptions.

a. The third-largest lake in Italy, and an island nation in the Indian Ocean.

b. A republic in the Russian Federation that borders Mongolia, and an island nation in the Pacific Ocean threatened by rising sea levels.

c. Two African countries, one of whose capitals is Niamey.

15 Pascal is a leading variety of which common vegetable? Known scientifically as *Apium graveolens*, it is a main ingredient of Waldorf salad.

Three bonus questions on French scientists

a. Born in 1778, which scientist discovered the law of combining volumes for ideal gases? He also devised, and gave his name to, a measure of alcohol by volume.

b. Henri Moissan received the 1906 Nobel Prize for Chemistry for the isolation of which element, the lightest halogen?

c. Which chemist played a leading role in establishing the oxygen theory of combustion? He was beheaded during the French Revolution.

16 The Pragmatic Sanction of 1713 aimed to secure the undisputed and undivided succession of the lands of which royal house?

Three bonus questions on royal houses

a. Who was the fifth British monarch of the House of Hanover?

b. Which year saw the accession of Britain's last Stuart ruler?

c. Which ruler, who acceded in 1100, is traditionally regarded as the last English king of the house of Normandy?

17 In 1917, 1944 and 1963 the Nobel Peace Prize was awarded to which organisation?

Three bonus questions on peace

a. 'Since wars begin in the minds of men, it is in the minds of men that the defences of peace must be constructed.' These are the opening words of the constitution of which agency of the United Nations?

b. From which congress did Benjamin Disraeli return in 1878, saying 'Lord Salisbury and myself have brought you back peace – but a peace, I hope, with honour'?

c. In 2011, which European leader said, 'No one should think a further half-century of peace and prosperity is assured. It isn't. That is why I say that if the euro fails, Europe will fail'?

18 Answer as soon as your name is called. Give the dictionary spelling of the container for holy objects known as a 'reliquary'.

Three bonus questions on the Venerable Bede

a. As exemplars for the clerics of his day, Bede cites St Aidan and which saint, born around 634? His tomb is at Durham Cathedral, which is dedicated to him.

b. In addition to their other merits, Bede's historical works are notable for popularising which dating system, devised by the Greek monk Dionysius the Short in the sixth century?

c. In the late ninth century, which king produced the first English version of Bede's *Ecclesiastical History*?

19 Quote: 'For our century, it is he who gave legitimacy to the implausible in the art of the novel.' These words of Milan Kundera refer to which literary figure, whose major works were published posthumously after he died from tuberculosis in Vienna in 1924?

Three bonus questions on pharmacology

a. Analgesics such as aspirin and ibuprofen are classified as NSAID; for what does this abbreviation stand?

b. Aspirin and ibuprofen work by inhibiting the enzymes COX-1 and COX-2. What is the full name of these enzymes?

c. Aspirin and ibuprofen are also antipyretic agents, meaning that they serve to reduce what condition?

20 In physics, what two-word term denotes the emission of electrons from a metal surface caused by incident light?

Three bonus questions on physics

a. A particle whose position x obeys the differential equation: $d^2x / dt^2 = -$ omega^2 x (d two x d t squared, equals minus omega squared x), is said to be executing what kind of motion?

b. In terms of omega, what is the frequency of oscillation of the particle?

c. An oscillator which is not oscillating in simple harmonic motion is known as what?

21 In his 1632 *Dialogue Concerning the Two Chief World Systems*, which natural philosopher described his principle of relativity using the example of the relative movement of the cargo on a ship sailing out of Venice?

Three bonus questions on scientific principles

a. Born in 1698, which French mathematician gives his name to the principle, also known as the least-action principle, that states that a particle moving between two points will follow the path along which its total action is as small as possible?

b. Named after a seventeenth-century French mathematician, which principle is a special case of the least-action principle applied to optics?

c. The principle allows the derivation of what type of equations named after two mathematicians, one Swiss and one Italian?

22 In the Royal Navy in the early twentieth century, what name, originally given to peas boiled in a bag, or pease pudding, came to be used for a junior officer or midshipman, and by association is now applied to any person who is given menial tasks?

Three bonus questions on diseases named after islands

a. Malta or Maltese fever is another name for which notifiable contagious disease, usually contracted by drinking infected milk or through close contact with infected animals?

b. Tangier disease, a rare inherited genetic condition characterised by very low HDL cholesterol levels, takes its name from an island in which North American bay, bounded by Maryland and Virginia?

c. Causing symptoms including fever and chest pain, Bornholm disease is an infection named after an island of which Nordic country where it was first observed in the 1930s?

23 'Ora opulenta' is a Latin translation of the name of which modern-day republic, whose 1949 constitution abolished the country's armed forces?

Three bonus questions on insect morphology

a. The respiratory system of insects consists of a series of tubes or tracheae. What term denotes the tracheae openings in the exoskeleton that allow for gas exchange?

b. What organs on the head of an insect consist of three parts: the scape, pedicel and flagellum?

c. Especially prominent in parasitic wasps, which egg-laying organ is found on the abdomen of female insects?

24 What given name links: a cousin of Jane Eyre in the novel by Charlotte Brontë; the only 'plain' Bennet daughter in Jane Austen's *Pride and Prejudice*, and the daughter of a trade unionist, the title character of an 1848 novel by Elizabeth Gaskell?

Three bonus questions on economics

a. In 1933, which British economist wrote an open letter to President Roosevelt in the *New York Times*, recommending government spending to reinvigorate the economy?

b. From 1933, Roosevelt implemented a package of state intervention and stimulus policies known by what popular name?

c. The Norwegian economist Ragnar Frisch made the distinction between the study of the behaviour of individuals and firms, and the study of the economy as a whole system. What term, also associated with Keynes, describes the latter approach?

25 'Fifteen orang-utans that look like London Mayor Boris Johnson' is one of the viral features of which self-styled 'social news organisation', created in 2006 by the MIT graduate Jonah Peretti?

Three bonus questions on opera

a. Meaning 'realism', the Italian opera style known as *verismo* is often said to have originated with the first performance, in 1892, of which opera by Pietro Mascagni?

b. Also in the *verismo* style, which opera by Leoncavallo is often performed as a double bill with *Cavalleria Rusticana*?

c. Which opera by Puccini is often cited as an example of *verismo*? Set in Rome, its title character is a singer, heartlessly tricked by the chief of police.

26 'The Trolley Song' and 'The Boy Next Door' are among songs performed by Judy Garland in which film of 1944, centring on the impending move by the Smith family to New York City in the days leading up to the 1904 World's Fair?

Three bonus questions on entries in *The Portable Flower-Garden*, a work of 1823 by the botanist Bess Kent. In each case, identify the common garden plant or flower from the author's description.

a. In Kent's words, which plant 'not only served to grace triumphant brows, mortal and immortal, but was also placed over the houses of sick persons, from some superstitious notion of its efficacy.'

b. 'It is connected with the sports of childhood and the pleasures of youth. It is a favourite with man, woman and child; it is the robin of flowers.'

c. 'One of the greatest pests to gardeners ... And yet it must be acknowledged that this little red and white flower is extremely beautiful and were it but a little more modest, would doubtless be a general favourite.'

27 What six-letter word denotes both the open-roofed entrance hall of an ancient Roman house and either of the two upper cavities of the heart from which blood is passed to the ventricles?

Three bonus questions on popular science

a. Which mathematician succeeded Richard Dawkins as the Simonyi Professor of the Public Understanding of Science at Oxford University?

b. Which 2003 book by Marcus du Sautoy is subtitled *Why an Unsolved Problem in Mathematics Matters*?

c. The discovery of the largest-known Mersenne prime in 2008 was rewarded with a prize from the Electronic Frontier Foundation as the first verified prime with more than how many digits?

28 'Excuse me if I speak English. We're about to draw the raffle tickets ... Have a safe journey home and don't get too drunk!' These are words from the brief victory speech of which British athlete, in the Champs Elysées in July 2012?

Three bonus questions on Paris architecture

a. Sharing his surname with a writer of fairy tales, which architect designed a new National Library of France along the banks of the Seine? Comprising four L-shaped glass skyscrapers, it was completed in 1995.

b. 'Jean is willing to jump in, and take on things, and try.' This was Frank Gehry's verdict on which architect, whose quai Branly museum opened in 2006?

c. The architect Ange-Jacques Gabriel designed the Place Louis XV, begun in 1755 and now known by what name?

29 Described as the 'the flag-bearer for the constellations of winter', which constellation contains the red giant Aldebaran, the Pleiades, and the Crab Nebula?

Three bonus questions on astronomy. In each case, give the name from the description; all three names begin with the same three letters.

a. The brightest star in the constellation Scorpius, a supergiant ten thousand times the luminosity of the Sun?

b. A faint constellation of the southern sky often abbreviated to 'Ant', and named after an air-pump?

c. Finally, an interacting pair of galaxies with long curved tails, pulled out by gravity during the pair's close encounter?

30 The name of which scholar of the Northern Renaissance is an anagram of a word meaning 'one who rubs or manipulates the muscles to relieve tension or pain'?

Three bonus questions on toothache

a. 'There was never yet philosopher / That could endure the toothache patiently'. These are the words of Leonato, the father of Hero, in which play by Shakespeare?

b. 'My curse upon thy venom'd stang, / That shoots my tortured gums alang'. These words open which poet's 'Address to the Toothache', probably written in the 1780s?

c.   'The man with toothache thinks everyone happy whose teeth are sound. The poverty stricken man makes the same mistake about the rich man.' These are the words of which Irish dramatist?

> 'It's against the zeitgeist,
> which is always a good idea.
> It's still there as an outpost of
> cleverness that celebrates people
> knowing things.'
>
> IAN HISLOP
> (Editor, *Private Eye*)
> Contestant, 2005

The Answers

1. Plato (in *The Republic*)
   a.   Chauvet Cave / Cave of Chauvet-Pont-d'Arc
   b.   *Grizzly Man*
   c.   Klaus Kinski

2. Maximilian (I)
   a.   The Hague / Den Haag
   b.   Tallinn
   c.   Valletta

3. 1974 (28 February–10 October)
   a.   Ripon
   b.   Stamford
   c.   Lichfield

4. 'Road'
   a.   The assassination of President John F. Kennedy
   b.   J.G. Ballard
   c.   Stephen King

5. Mongolia (still shown as Chinese territory on some maps published in Taiwan)
   a.   Westward Ho!
   b.   *Oliver!*
   c.   'Help!' by The Beatles

6. Kaleidoscope (Greek: *kalos*, 'beautiful'; *eidos*, 'form')
   a.   Amphora

b. Plethora

c. Agora

7 273 (degrees Celsius; using Charles' law; this is because minus 273 degrees Celsius is absolute zero, or zero degrees kelvin)

    a. 8

    b. Compression factor / compressibility factor

    c. Virial (coefficients)

8 Historic Places

    a. Somalia (Mozambique 2,470 km; Egypt 2,450 km; Madagascar 4,828 km but is not on the African continent)

    b. Togo (56km; Benin is slightly longer, at 121 km)

    c. (Democratic Republic of) Congo

9 *Far from the Madding Crowd* (the film is set in the Dorset village of Ewedown)

    a. Rio de Janeiro

    b. Philippines

    c. Florida (Santa Fe, New Mexico was founded in 1610)

10 A.C. (Grayling, Benson, Nielsen, Milan)

    a. Spiral and Elliptical

    b. Dwarf spheroidal

    c. Ultra-Luminous InfraRed Galaxy

11 Matrix

    a. Gram staining / Gram's stain (Hans Christian Gram, 1850–1938)

    b. Purple (accept violet or purple-blue)

    c. Iodine

12 *Tender Is the Night*

    a. Sherry

    b. La Mancha

    c. Rioja

13 The Magic Circle
- **a.** Archimedes
- **b.** (Isaac) Newton
- **c.** 11.001 (accept 11001)

14 Tautology / repetition of an element ('Hill Hill Hill', 'Isle of Sheep Island', 'River River')
- **a.** Como and Comoros
- **b.** Tuva and Tuvalu
- **c.** Niger and Nigeria

15 Celery
- **a.** (Joseph Louis) Gay-Lussac (abv is referred to as 'degrees Gay-Lussac' in some countries)
- **b.** Fluorine
- **c.** (Antoine-Laurent de) Lavoisier

16 Hapsburg
- **a.** William IV
- **b.** 1702 (Queen Anne, of course)
- **c.** Henry I

17 (International) Red Cross
- **a.** UNESCO (United Nations Educational, Scientific, and Cultural Organization)
- **b.** (Congress of) Berlin (after the Russo-Turkish War, 1877–1878)
- **c.** Angela Merkel

18 R-e-l-i-q-u-a-r-y
- **a.** St Cuthbert
- **b.** AD / BC (accept either, adding the other)
- **c.** Alfred (the Great)

19 (Franz) Kafka
- **a.** Non-Steroidal Anti-Inflammatory Drugs

    b.   Cyclooxygenase (one and two)

    c.   Fever

20 Photoelectric effect

    a.   Simple harmonic motion (accept S.H.M., giving all three words)

    b.   Omega / 2*pi (omega over two pi)

    c.   Anharmonic (oscillator)

21 Galileo (Galilei)

    a.   (Pierre-Louis de) Maupertuis (1698–1759)

    b.   Fermat's principle (Pierre de Fermat, c.1601–1665)

    c.   Euler-Lagrange equations (Leonhard Euler, Joseph Lagrange)

22 Dogsbody

    a.   Brucellosis or undulant fever

    b.   Chesapeake Bay

    c.   Denmark

23 Costa Rica

    a.   Spiracles

    b.   Antenna(e)

    c.   Ovipositor

24 Mary (Rivers / Bennet / Barton)

    a.   John Maynard Keynes

    b.   The New Deal

    c.   Macroeconomics

25 Buzzfeed

    a.   *Cavalleria Rusticana / Rustic Chivalry*

    b.   *Pagliacci / The Clowns*

    c.   *Tosca*

26 *Meet Me in St Louis*

    a.   Bay (bay laurel, *Laurus nobilis*)
    b.   Daisy
    c.   Convolvulus (bindweed)

27 Atrium
    a.   Marcus du Sautoy
    b.   *The Music of the Primes*
    c.   10 million (there are still prizes on offer for Mersenne primes of 100 million and 1 billion digits)

28 (Sir) Bradley Wiggins
    a.   (Dominique) Perrault (Charles Perrault, 1628–1703, was the author)
    b.   (Jean) Nouvel
    c.   Place de la Concorde

29 Taurus
    a.   Antares
    b.   Antlia
    c.   Antennae / Antenna galaxies

30 Erasmus ('masseur', of course)
    a.   *Much Ado about Nothing*
    b.   Robert Burns
    c.   George Bernard Shaw ('Maxims for Revolutionists' in *Man and Superman*, 1903)

Match Twelve

1 Answer as soon as your name is called. Add the number of the current French Republic to the number of permanent members of the UN Security Council. What number results?

Three bonus questions on a preserve

a. According to the Oxford English Dictionary, which preserve was originally 'a sweet, solid quince jelly flavoured by rose water and musk or ambergris, and cut into squares for eating'?

b. The name 'marmalade' is derived from *marmelo*, the word for quince in the language of which country, from which most of the early imports of both the fruit and the preserve came to Britain?

c. The fruit *Citrus aurantium*, now most often used in the manufacture of marmalade, is commonly known by what name?

2 Give the common two-word name of the Asian country whose full name is sometimes abbreviated to DPRK.

Three bonus questions on physics

a. The physicist Andre Geim of the University of Manchester is the only person so far to have won both a Nobel Prize and what other award, which he received in 2000 for an experiment on a frog?

b. Geim shared the 2000 Physics Ig Nobel Prize for levitating a frog using a superconducting magnet, an effect that relied on what physical property of the water in the frog?

c. The Physics Ig Nobel Prize for 2011 recognised research into the side effects of two athletic events, one of which often induces dizziness while the other does not, despite having an apparently similar action. Name both events.

3 Listen carefully and answer as soon as your name is called. Take the word 'machine' and discount those letters that are not roman numerals. What four-digit decimal number is represented by the remainder?

Three bonus questions on a film director

a. 'His flamboyant style and unorthodox biographies of musical notables have divided viewers into outraged observers or staunch followers.' These words in *Chambers Biographical Dictionary* refer to which British film director, who died in 2011?

b. Described in his own words as 'the story of the marriage between a homosexual and a nymphomaniac', Russell's 1970 film *The Music Lovers* depicts the life of which nineteenth-century composer?

c. Glenda Jackson won the Academy Award for Best Actress in which Ken Russell film of 1969, based on a novel by D.H. Lawrence?

4 *Falciparum* and *vivax* are among species of a protozoan genus that causes which disease?

Three bonus questions on battlefields in Scotland

a. Site of a decisive defeat for Edward II's English army in 1314, Bannockburn is a village immediately south of which city of central Scotland?

b. Site of a battle during the Jacobite rebellion of 1689, the pass of Killiecrankie is around thirty miles north of which royal burgh on the River Tay?

c. Giving its name to the final battle of the Jacobite rebellion of 1745–1746, the village of Culloden is a few miles east of which city?

5 The author of the 1875 work *L'Uomo Delinquente*, which Italian physician is best known for his theory of anthropological criminology, postulating the existence of a recognisable criminal 'type'?

> **Three bonus questions on two-word terms that sound like a combination of an educational institution and a common surname and so, if they were starter questions, could just possibly be answered by Roger Tilling alone – for example, 'Newcastle, Brown!' or 'Lincoln, Greene!' Got it?**

a. Associated with jewellery, an alloy in which element number 47 makes up at least 92.5 per cent of the content?

b. The European Cup winners in 1979 and 1980?

c. A manufacturer of luxury sports cars, especially associated with the 1964 film *Goldfinger*?

6 'In this twenty-fifth year of his rule, eminent men are intoning a chorus of praise to him as the great peace lord of the world.' These words, from a special commemorative section of the *New York Times* in 1913, refer to which monarch?

Three bonus questions on an Italian noblewoman

a. An inspiration for numerous literary works, what was the given name of the young woman who was beheaded on the orders of Pope Clement VIII in 1599 for the murder of her abusive father, Francesco Cenci?

b. Born in Bologna in 1579, which Baroque artist is noted for a painting of Beatrice now in the Galleria Nazionale in Rome? His works include the ceiling fresco *Aurora*.

c. Reni's painting of Beatrice is thought to have been the inspiration for *The Cenci*, a verse tragedy of 1819 by which Romantic poet?

7 'We all know that art is not truth. Art is a lie that makes us realise truth.' These are the words of which Spanish painter, born in 1881?

Three bonus questions on British history

a. Ennobled in 1918, the Conservative George Cave became the last member of the House of Lords to hold which great office of state?

b. Who was the last member of the House of Lords to have been foreign secretary? He resigned in 1982.

c. Who was the last person to remain a peer throughout his time as prime minister? His last term was from 1895 to 1902.

8 Answer as soon as your name is called. What comes next in this sequence, being the countries that border Austria, in clockwise order: Germany, Czech Republic, Slovakia, Hungary and which country?

Three bonus questions on Pacific island nations. In each case, give the country that includes the following islands.

    a. First, for five points: Beru, Tarawa and Christmas Island?

    b. Second: Guadalcanal, Santa Isabel and Malaita?

    c. Finally: Viti Levu and Vanua Levu?

9 What five-letter term denotes both a colourless volatile liquid, and a substance that was once thought to fill the universe and through which light and radio waves travelled? It is now often used figuratively in the latter sense.

Three bonus questions on an institution

    a. Established through the Constitutional Reform Act of 2005, what body came into existence on 1 October 2009 to replace the Appellate Committee of the House of Lords?

    b. The Supreme Court is based in which early twentieth-century Neo-Gothic building on Parliament Square, opposite the Palace of Westminster?

    c. Of the first twelve Supreme Court justices to be appointed, who was the only woman?

10 From the Greek meaning 'between the rivers', what is the ancient name for the area of land between the Tigris and the Euphrates?

Three bonus questions on religious texts

    a. The Rigveda, a large collection of hymns composed during the second millennium BCE, is the oldest known text in which language?

   b.   Related to Sanskrit, in what language are the earliest
            texts of Southern Buddhism? It developed in Northern
            India from the fifth century BCE.

   c.   Ardha Magadhi or 'Half Magadhi' is a principal language
            of the texts of which Indian religion?

11 'I completely wreck and sack Woking, then proceed via
Kingston and Richmond to London, selecting South
Kensington for feats of peculiar atrocity.' These are the
words of which author in the plan for one of his novels,
published in book form in 1898?

Three bonus questions on Anglo-Saxon literature

   a.   Meaning 'knowing', what term denotes a type of
            metaphorical phrase often used in Anglo-Saxon poetry,
            such as 'the whale's road', meaning 'the sea'?

   b.   In *Beowulf*, the line 'that [sword] edge was not useless to
            the warrior now' is an example of what figure of speech,
            defined as an ironic negative understatement?

   c.   Which English city gives its name to the book of Anglo-
            Saxon poetry which includes 'The Wanderer' and 'The
            Seafarer', and also contains over ninety riddles?

12 '555' in Thai, 'asg' in Swedish and 'mdr' in French are
equivalents of which three-letter internet abbreviation,
defined by the OED as something that is used to draw
attention to a joke or to express amusement?

Three bonus questions on internet deception

   a.   After a type of toy, what name is given to internet users
            who, for deceptive purposes, log on to a message board
            or other web community under an assumed name?

   b.   Widely reproduced since its 1993 publication in the
            New Yorker, a cartoon by Peter Steiner states that 'On

the internet, nobody knows that you're ...' what?

c. Author of *A People's Tragedy: A History of the Russian Revolution*, which historian admitted posting anonymously written derogatory reviews of his rivals' books on Amazon in April 2010?

⑬ When *The Hornet's Nest* went on sale in 2003, which Nobel laureate became the first person to be both a published novelist and a former president of the USA?

Three bonus questions on mountain peaks

a. What is the literal meaning of the French term *aiguille*, used for a sharply pointed rock outcrop or mountain peak, and often applied to pinnacles that are the products of frost action?

b. The Aiguille du Géant and Aiguille du Midi are peaks in which mountain massif in the Alps, lying along the French-Italian border and reaching into Switzerland?

c. Comprising three sharp, jagged peaks more than 2,500 metres high, the Torres del Paine are around 300 kilometres north of Punta Arenas in which Latin American country?

⑭ Illuminating the Witch Head Nebula, which blue giant star in the constellation of Orion is one of the ten brightest in the night sky?

Three bonus questions on mythological subjects in the collection of the Manchester City Art Gallery

a. Who is the title figure of an 1888 work by Lord Frederic Leighton? Enslaved and dressed in black, she waits her turn at the well, her husband having been killed by Achilles during the Trojan War.

b. In a work by John William Waterhouse, which companion of Hercules is depicted being seduced by nymphs while in search of water for the Argonauts?

c. In another work by Lord Leighton, who is shown watching in vain over the Hellespont for her lover, Leander?

15 What word can follow the names Nusselt, Grashof, Weber and Froude to give a dimensionless physical quantity?

Three bonus questions on lines of latitude

a. The Tropic of Cancer passes within twenty miles of two Asian capital cities. Dhaka, in Bangladesh, is one; what is the other, the capital of Oman?

b. Which of the capital cities of South America lies closest to the Tropic of Capricorn, at around 120 miles south of the line?

c. Which of the capital cities of South America lies closest to the Equator?

16 The adjective 'phrenic' refers to what part of the human body that takes the form of a thin, membranous dome-shaped muscle?

Three bonus questions on mammalian physiology

a. Comprising Bowman's capsule, convoluted tubule and loop of Henle, what is the basic structural and functional unit of the kidney?

b. Receiving blood from an afferent renal arteriole, what name is given to the network of capillaries in Bowman's capsule?

c. What term denotes the fine muscular ducts that propel urine from the kidneys to the bladder?

17 Which country house is this? Lying a few miles west of Chipping Sodbury in Gloucestershire, it gives its name to an eighteenth-century cabinet that became the most expensive piece of furniture ever sold when it fetched £19 million at auction in 2004? A prominent venue for equestrian trials, it also gives its name to an Olympic racquet sport.

Three bonus questions on ancient art

a. In which country is Blombos Cave, the site of the discovery of several pieces of engraved ochre that date to before 75,000 BC?

b. Discovered in the 1860s, which cave in the Spanish region of Cantabria contains rock paintings that date to around 14,000 BC?

c. Which cave in the Dordogne region of France is also noted for its prehistoric rock paintings discovered by accident by a group of children in 1940?

18 Which work of 2007 by the Canadian author and social activist Naomi Klein is a critique of neo-liberalism that claims to expose how free-market policies have been imposed by exploiting upheaval and catastrophe around the world?

Three bonus questions on films based on works of journalism

a. Later revealed to be largely the invention of its author, the British journalist Nik Cohn was the author of a 1976 *New York* magazine piece which formed the basis for which film?

b. Which 1984 film about Cambodia's Khmer Rouge came out of the article 'The Death and Life of Dith Pran' by Sydney Schanberg of the *New York Times*?

c. The screenwriter Charlie Kaufman used *The Orchid Thief* by the *New Yorker* writer Susan Orlean as the basis for which film, starring Nicolas Cage as identical twins?

19 In meteorology, what does a Robinson Cup anemometer measure?

Three bonus questions on sea areas of the shipping forecast. In each case, name the area that borders the following.

a. First, for five points: Sole, Fastnet and Rockall?

b. Second: Fisher, Dogger and Humber?

c. Finally: Fair Isle, Forties and Forth?

20 Which year saw the birth of the mathematician Alfred North Whitehead, the death of Albert, the Prince Consort, the abolition of serfdom in Russia, and the start of the American Civil War?

Three bonus questions on gases

a. Which British scientist gave his name to the law formulated in 1803, which stated that the solubility of a gas in a liquid is directly proportional to the pressure of the gas?

b. One mole of ideal gas at a temperature of 15.5 degrees Celsius and a pressure of 1 bar has a volume of 24 litres. What is the volume, in litres, of 2 moles of gas at a pressure of 3 bar, at the same temperature?

c. What gas is produced by adding water to calcium carbide?

21 Born in 1832, which Russian art collector gives his name to a major art gallery in Moscow, especially noted for its collection of ikons?

Three bonus questions on a family

a. 'The Blessed Damozel' and 'The Prince's Progress' are nineteenth-century poems written by a brother and sister, respectively, with what surname?

b. Dante Gabriel Rossetti married which of his models in 1860, less than two years before her death from an overdose of laudanum?

c. 'Figs to fill your mouth, / Citrons from the south, / Sweet to tongue and sound to eye; / Come buy, come buy.' These are lines from which narrative poem by Christina Rossetti, illustrated by her brother in its 1862 edition?

22 Begun during the reign of Vespasian in around AD 70–72, which elliptical structure is said to have taken its name from the giant statue of Nero that stood nearby in the Via Sacra?

Three bonus questions on Roman officials

a. Discontinued in 22 BC, which magistrate's original function of registering citizens and their property was later greatly expanded to include supervision of moral conduct?

b. From a Latin word meaning 'set in authority', what term denoted various military and civil officials in ancient Rome, the highest-ranking of which virtually directed the Empire's civil administration?

c. In the Republic, what title was given to a temporary magistrate with extraordinary powers granted in times of military and, later, internal crises?

23 Formed in 1973, the Polisario Front is a politico-military organisation dedicated to ending Moroccan control of which former Spanish territory?

Three bonus questions on aspiring nations

a. Promised but not granted a homeland after the First World War, which people inhabit a contiguous territory divided between Iran, Syria, Iraq and Turkey?

b. Italy's Lega Nord gives which name to the area around the Po Valley? In 1996, the party's founder, Umberto Bossi, declared it an 'independent republic'.

c. Supporters of the 'Republic of Cascadia' wish to unite Washington State and Oregon with which Canadian province?

24 In party political terms, what links Reginald Prentice in 1977, Peter Thurnham in 1996, Shaun Woodward in 1999 and Quentin Davies in 2007?

Three bonus questions on the novels of Alexandre Dumas, père

a. Which novel by Dumas interweaves the fictional story of the horticulturalist Cornelius van Baerle with the historical events that surrounded the murder of two Dutch statesman in 1672?

b. Which novel by Dumas begins with the St Bartholomew's Day Massacre of the Huguenots in 1572, and ends with the death of Charles IX in 1574?

c. *Twenty Years Later* and *The Viscount of Bragelonne* were the sequels to which of Dumas' novels, first serialised in 1844?

25 The 'puddling process', patented by Henry Cort in 1784, subjects pig iron to heat and frequent stirring in a furnace in the presence of oxidising substances to convert it into what other form of iron?

Three bonus questions on chemistry

a. What Greek-derived term denotes elements in Group 17 of the Periodic Table? They have seven electrons in their outer shells and are highly reactive non-metals.

b. Which of the halogens has an atomic number of nine? It is the most electronegative element known, and hence is a highly reactive oxidising agent.

c. Which of the halogens is found in the hormone thyroxine?

26 In which regular polygon is the internal angle at each vertex 135 degrees, and the sum of all the internal angles 1,080 degrees?

Three bonus questions on mathematics

a. Renowned for his list of problems posed at the 1900 International Congress of Mathematicians, which German mathematician gives his name to a complete inner product space?

b. A concatenation of the Greek for 'straight' and 'angled', what word is used to describe two points in a Hilbert space whose inner product is zero?

c. Which well-known theorem of geometry generalises to all Hilbert spaces, where it asserts that the squared norm of the sum of two orthogonal vectors is equal to the sum of their squared norms?

27 In his book *Pudd'nhead Wilson,* Mark Twain wrote that which vegetable is 'nothing but cabbage with a college education'?

Three bonus questions on feasts

a. Its Greek-derived name meaning 'manifestation', which feast day of the Christian calendar follows Twelfth Night?

b. What is the Hebrew name for the Jewish 'Feast of Lots', celebrated in February or March and commemorating the deliverance of the Jews from a massacre planned by the Persian vizier Haman?

c. The Celtic religious festival Lughnasadh, the feast of the god Lugh, is celebrated in which month, on the same date as the Christian Lammas Day?

28 So named because of an invasion by Allied forces in April 1915, Anzac Cove is a coastal feature of which peninsula in Western Turkey?

Three bonus questions on place names

a. Kingston, Jamaica was named in honour of which British monarch who had come to the throne three years before the city was founded in 1692?

b. The sixteenth-century Portuguese explorer Lourenço Marques gave his name to a southern African capital now known by what name?

c. The market town in central France formerly known as La Haye en Touraine was renamed in the early nineteenth century in honour of which philosopher, born there in 1596?

29 What adjective may precede 'conditioning', when referring to Pavlov; 'economics', when referring to the work of Ricardo and Mill; and 'mechanics' when referring to Sir Isaac Newton?

Three bonus questions on agencies of the European Union

a. Formerly the Public Health Executive Agency, the EAHC is the Executive Agency for Health and – what?

b. Based in Lithuania, the EIGE is the European Institute for what?

c. Its programmes including 'Marco Polo', which seeks to find alternatives to road transport, the EACI is the European Agency for Competitiveness and what?

30 What three words does the acronym 'RIB' represent, when it refers to a small open vessel with a fibreglass hull and rubber sides?

Three bonus questions on words that can be typed using only the middle row of characters on a standard QWERTY keyboard. In each case, give the word from the description.

a. The 'pure knight' of Arthurian legend; in Malory's work he is the son of Lancelot and Elaine.

b. A leguminous fodder crop with clover-like leaves; it is also known as lucerne.

c. The US state whose settlements include Sitka, Ketchikan and Fairbanks?

The Answers

1 Ten (five and five, of course)
  - **a.** Marmalade
  - **b.** Portugal (the word for 'quince' is different in other Romance languages)
  - **c.** Seville (or bitter) orange

2 North Korea (full name: Democratic People's Republic of Korea)
  - **a.** Ig Nobel Prize
  - **b.** Diamagnetism (creates magnetic field in opposition to externally applied magnetic field)
  - **c.** Discus and hammer (discus induces dizziness)

3 1,101 (i.e. MCI)
  - **a.** Ken Russell
  - **b.** Tchaikovsky
  - **c.** *Women in Love* (not *The Rainbow*, which Russell filmed in 1989, also starring Jackson)

4 Malaria (the genus being *Plasmodium*)
  - **a.** Stirling
  - **b.** Perth
  - **c.** Inverness

5 (Cesare) Lombroso
  - **a.** Sterling silver
  - **b.** Nottingham Forest (NB not Aston Villa, who won in 1982)
  - **c.** Aston Martin

6 (Kaiser) Wilhelm II (accept 'the Kaiser')
- **a.** Beatrice
- **b.** (Guido) Reni
- **c.** Shelley

7 (Pablo) Picasso
- **a.** Home Secretary
- **b.** (Lord) Carrington
- **c.** (Marquess of) Salisbury

8 Slovenia
- **a.** Kiribati
- **b.** Solomon Islands
- **c.** Fiji

9 Ether
- **a.** The Supreme Court (of the United Kingdom)
- **b.** Middlesex Guildhall
- **c.** Baroness Hale (of Richmond) / Lady Hale (Brenda Marjorie Hale)

10 Mesopotamia
- **a.** Sanskrit
- **b.** Pali
- **c.** Jainism

11 H.G. Wells (*The War of the Worlds*, of course)
- **a.** Kenning
- **b.** Litotes
- **c.** Exeter (the Exeter Book, *Codex Exoniensis*)

12 Lol / laugh out loud ('five' in Thai is *ha*; *Asgarv*; *mort de rire*)
- **a.** Sock puppet / sock puppetry
- **b.** '... a dog'
- **c.** Orlando Figes

13 Jimmy Carter (2003 being the year of its American publication)
- **a.** Needle
- **b.** Mont blanc (Aiguille du Géant also known as Dent du Géant – Giant's Tooth)
- **c.** Chile

14 Rigel / Beta Orionis
- **a.** Andromache (*Captive Andromache*)
- **b.** Hylas (*Hylas and the Nymphs*, 1896)
- **c.** Hero (*The Last Watch of Hero*)

15 Number
- **a.** Muscat
- **b.** Asuncion (in Paraguay)
- **c.** Quito (in Ecuador)

16 Diaphragm (Latin: *phrenicus*; it can also relate to mental activity but that doesn't answer the question)
- **a.** Nephron
- **b.** Glomerulus
- **c.** Ureter(s) (not urethra, which connects the urinary bladder to the genitals)

17 Badminton (House)
- **a.** South Africa
- **b.** Altamira
- **c.** Lascaux

18 *The Shock Doctrine* (*: The Rise of Disaster Capitalism*)
- **a.** *Saturday Night Fever* ('Tribal Rites of the New Saturday Night')
- **b.** *The Killing Fields*
- **c.** *Adaptation*

19 Wind speed / wind pressure
- **a.** Shannon

    b.   German Bight

    c.   Cromarty

20 1861

    a.   (William) Henry (1774–1836; Henry's law)

    b.   16 litres (24×2/3; 15.5 0 c, pressure 1 bar)

    c.   Ethyne / acetylene

21 (Pavel) Tretyakov

    a.   Rossetti (Dante Gabriel and Christina)

    b.   Elizabeth (or Lizzie) Siddal

    c.   *Goblin Market*

22 Colosseum / Flavian Amphitheatre (in Rome)

    a.   Censor

    b.   Prefect (Latin: *praeficare*)

    c.   Dictator (originally named *magister populi*)

23 Western Sahara

    a.   Kurds

    b.   Padania

    c.   British Columbia

24 All 'crossed the floor' / defected from one party to another (Labour to Tory, Tory to Lib Dem, Tory to Labour, Tory to Labour, respectively; accept similar)

    a.   *The Black Tulip*

    b.   *La reine Margot / The Queen Margot*

    c.   *The Three Musketeers*

25 Wrought iron

    a.   Halogens

    b.   Fluorine

    c.   Iodine

26 Octagon

a. (David) Hilbert (1862–1943)
b. Orthogonal (not 'perpendicular' which does not fit the etymology; Greek: *ortho* and *gonios*)
c. Pythagoras' theorem / the Pythagorean theorem

27 Cauliflower
a. (Feast of) Epiphany (Twelfth Night is strictly the evening of 5 January, the eve of the Epiphany)
b. Purim
c. August (1 August in the northern hemisphere, 1 February in the southern)

28 Gallipoli
a. William III / William of Orange
b. Maputo
c. (René) Descartes (formerly La Haye-Descartes; in 1967, officially abbreviated to Descartes)

29 Classical
a. Consumers
b. Gender Equality
c. Innovation

30 Rigid Inflatable Boat
a. Galahad
b. Alfalfa
c. Alaska

Match Thirteen

1 *Sus scrofa* is the scientific name for which domesticated mammal, breeds of which include the Duroc, Landrace, Spotted and Large White?

Three bonus questions on fictional pigs

a. In a series of stories by P.G. Wodehouse, what is the name of the prize-winning pig owned by Lord Emsworth?

b. Described as 'majestic-looking ... with a wise and benevolent appearance', which pig in George Orwell's *Animal Farm* dies three days after organising the first meeting of the animals?

c. What is the name of the porcine title character in Dick King-Smith's 1983 book *The Sheep-Pig*?

2 The Strait of Bonifacio separates the northern end of the Italian island of Sardinia from which other island?

Three bonus questions on the year 1555

a. Name either of the two Anglican bishops who were burned at the stake at Oxford in 1555 as part of the Marian persecutions?

b. Which Bavarian city gives its name to a treaty of 1555 that made the legal division of Christendom permanent within the Holy Roman Empire?

c. In 1555, which ruler began abdicating his titles? He retired to a monastery in Spain the following year.

3 *A Moment of War* by Laurie Lee, *For Whom the Bell Tolls* by Ernest Hemingway and *Homage to Catalonia* by George Orwell are all works concerned with which twentieth-century conflict?

Three bonus questions on winners of the Man Booker Prize. In each case, name the country of birth that links the authors of the following novels.

a. *Vernon God Little*, *Schindler's Ark* and *Oscar and Lucinda*?

b. *The Sea*, *The Gathering* and *The Sea, The Sea*?

c. *The Inheritance of Loss*, *The God of Small Things* and *The White Tiger*?

4 Listen carefully and answer as soon as your name is called. In the words of the well-known Christmas song, if 'colly birds' to the power 'French hens' is '64', what is 'gold rings' to the power 'turtle doves'?

Three bonus questions on existentialism

a. Which French philosopher's maxim 'existence precedes essence' has been described as the most succinct statement of existentialism?

b. Sometimes described as one of the founders of existentialism, which German philosopher's works include *Reason and Existenz* (sic)? Persecuted by the Nazis, he remained in Germany until after the war.

c. Born in Copenhagen in 1813, who is the first modern philosopher to be commonly described as an existentialist?

5 The addition of what letter of the alphabet transforms the name of a seaport at the mouth of the Red Sea into that of a former German state paired with Wurttemberg after the Second World War?

Three bonus questions on pairs of words whose spelling differs only in the substitution of a final letter 'l' for a letter 'r', for example 'brother' and 'brothel'. In each case, give both words from the definitions.

a. An item of movable property, and a verb meaning 'to engage in rapid, inconsequential talk'?

b. A small or squalid dwelling, and the collective noun for a group of trout or a verb meaning 'to rest on a cushion of air'?

c. A divine messenger, and an abstract noun meaning 'hot displeasure', 'wrath' or 'annoyance'?

6 Which country shares land frontiers with Iraq, Jordan, Kuwait, Oman, Yemen and Qatar?

Three bonus questions on the art critic Robert Hughes

a. Robert Hughes's 1987 work *The Fatal Shore* is a history of the settlement of which country, the place of his birth?

b. What was the title of Robert Hughes's account of modern art, which appeared both in print and as a television series in 1980?

c. Born in 1746, which Spanish artist is the subject of a 2003 biography by Robert Hughes?

7 Which short novel of the late 1890s begins with ghost stories being told on Christmas Eve? It features the apparent apparitions of two servants, the valet Peter Quint and the former governess Miss Jessel, who both worked at the country house of Bly.

Three bonus questions on an American novelist

a. *Telegraph Avenue* is a novel of 2012 by which author, who won the Pulitzer Prize for *The Amazing Adventures of Kavalier and Clay*?

b. Michael Douglas played the college professor and hopelessly 'blocked' writer Grady Tripp in the 2000 film of which novel by Chabon?

c. Chabon's Hugo Award-winning counter-factual history *The Yiddish Policemen's Union* imagined a Jewish homeland that had been created in which present-day US state?

8 The 2012 Royal Society Summer Science Exhibition featured a display of which former landmass between Scotland, Denmark and the Channel Islands? Flooded by ice melt thousands of years ago, it is named after a large sandbank in the North Sea.

Three bonus questions on terminology used in the Shipping Forecast, according to the glossary on the Met Office website

a. According to the glossary, 'soon' means 'expected within six to twelve hours of time of issue'. What word means 'expected within six hours of time of issue'?

b. What present participle is defined as 'the changing of the wind in the opposite direction to veering', for example, south-east to north-east?

   c. What short word is used to describe visibility of more than five nautical miles?

9 Whose law states that equal volumes of two gases at the same temperature and pressure contain the same number of molecules?

Three bonus questions on human skin

   a. In a homograft, skin is grafted from one person to another, usually as a temporary healing measure. What is the name of the procedure in which skin for a graft is taken from another part of the body of the patient?

   b. Taken from that of a seventeenth-century Italian physiologist, what name is given to the innermost layer of the skin's epidermis?

   c. Which glands in the skin open into hair follicles?

10 Which fourth-century Bishop of Myra had a reputation as a miracle worker, including raising to life three boys after they were murdered in a brine-tub? He became the patron saint of children, sailors, unmarried girls, merchants, pawnbrokers, apothecaries, perfumiers and of Russia.

Three bonus questions on Dublin

   a. Sackville Street in Dublin was, in 1924, renamed in honour of which nationalist leader of the early nineteenth century?

   b. Now a museum, which gaol near Phoenix Park is particularly associated with the struggle for Irish independence, its inmates having included Parnell, Michael Davitt and Eamon de Valera?

c. Which nineteenth-century building became a symbol of the 1916 Easter Rising? Having been seized by insurgents, the proclamation of the Irish Republic was read out from its steps.

11 Identify the play by Shakespeare in which these lines appear: 'Some say that ever 'gainst that season comes / Wherein our saviour's birth is celebrated, / This bird of dawning singeth all night long; / And then, they say, no spirit dare stir abroad.'

Three bonus questions on flowers in Shakespeare

a. In *A Midsummer Night's Dream*, Oberon's speech 'I know a bank where the wild thyme blows' also refers to which flower, a member of the rose family sometimes known as sweet briar?

b. In the same speech, Shakespeare rhymes 'eglantine' with the name of which flower, a species of honeysuckle which Oberon describes as 'luscious'?

c. The same speech also refers to which flower, noted for its colouring and sometimes known as 'heartsease', which Oberon describes as 'nodding'?

12 What two-digit number links: the *Capricci* written by Paganini between 1801 and 1807 for unaccompanied violin; the number of books in the Iliad; the cinema industry standard for filming frames per second; and the number of carats representing pure gold?

Three bonus questions on words that begin with the letters 't.r.i.' but have no connection with the number three. In each case, give the word from the definition.

a. The study of the interaction of sliding surfaces, including friction, lubrication and bearings?

    b. The study of the hair and scalp?

    c. In ancient Rome, a legionary officer or an official who represented the Plebeians?

13 The prosaically named Statute Law Revision Act of 1863 repealed a large number of the provisions of which constitutional document, dating to the reign of King John?

Three bonus questions on George Bernard Shaw

    a. Give the two words that complete this observation by Shaw in *The Apple Cart*: 'What Englishman will give his mind to politics as long as he can afford to keep a ...' what?

    b. What, according to Shaw in *The Devil's Disciple*, is 'the only way in which a man can become famous without ability'?

    c. In *Man and Superman*, Shaw says that what form of government 'substitutes election by the incompetent many, for appointment by the corrupt few'?

14 Listen carefully. After Russia and Canada, what is the next country with a larger land area than any single one of its neighbours?

Three bonus questions on names

    a. What name, thought to denote a dog-like or churlish manner, was given to a member of the school of Greek philosophy which included Diogenes of Sinope?

    b. Said to contain 'the most unsociable and unclubable men in London', the Diogenes Club was co-founded by which fictional character?

c. What is the common name of the crustaceans to which the genus 'diogenes' belongs, noted for their use of the shells of other animals to protect their soft abdomens?

15 'Yellow Mountain Fur Peak', 'Spring Snail', 'Big Red Robe', 'Dragon Well' and 'Iron Goddess' are among names that appear in Chinese lists of the 'ten most notable' varieties of what agricultural product?

Three bonus questions on place names and their anagrams. In each case, give both words from the explanation or definition.

a. 'A large North African country', and 'the insignia of royalty, for example, the crown, sceptre and orb'?

b. 'A town in Massachusetts that gives its name to a prominent liberal arts college', and 'a burrowing rodent with large cheek pouches'?

c. 'A state of north-east India noted for the production of tea', and 'to gather together or accumulate, for example, a fortune or library'?

16 What final four letters link the English names of countries whose emblems are a golden lion wielding a sword, a white eagle with a golden beak and talons, a white cross on a red field, and a harp?

Three bonus questions on shorter words that can be made using any of the six letters of the word 'empire'. In each case, give the word from the definition.

a. An adjective meaning 'stiffly formal' or 'prudishly disapproving'?

b. A French word meaning 'worse', a comparative of the adjective 'mauvais'?

c. A title of high office in Islamic countries, for example, the monarch of Kuwait or Qatar?

17 In chemistry, what would be the colour of a phenolphthalein solution at a pH of above 9.6?

Three bonus questions on chemical elements

a. Named after a village in Scotland, which Group 2 element was formerly used in sugar refining and is still used in the manufacture of fireworks?

b. Of the elements with no stable isotopes, which has the lowest atomic number?

c. Often used in steel alloys along with chromium, which element appears between technetium and niobium on the Periodic Table?

18 Which two geological periods lie on either side of the event known as the K-T extinction, at which non-avian dinosaurs disappeared? It occurred around 65 million years ago.

Three bonus questions on scientific terms beginning with the prefix 'syn-'. In each case, give the word from the definition.

a. In geology, a trough or fold of stratified rock in which the strata slope upwards from the axis?

b. In automotive engineering, a system of gear changing in which the driving and driven gear wheels revolve at the same speed during engagement by means of friction clutches?

c. In anatomy, a junction between two nerve cells, in the form of a minute gap across which impulses can pass?

19 MERLIN, now known as e-MERLIN, is an array of radio telescopes distributed around the UK and connected by an optical fibre network to which observatory in Cheshire?

Three bonus questions on astronomy

a. With an apparent visual magnitude of minus 1.44, the star Alpha Canis Majoris is more commonly known by what name?

b. With an apparent magnitude of plus 3.5, which sun-like star only twelve light years from our solar system has been a popular setting for science fiction, appearing in works by Isaac Asimov and Ursula Le Guin?

c. Stellar magnitudes form a negative logarithmic scale of brightness, so adding one to the magnitude corresponds to a certain factor decrease in light flux. What factor of decrease is given by adding five magnitudes, the approximate difference between Sirius and Tau Ceti?

20 'Your representative owes you, not his industry only, but his judgment; and he betrays instead of serving you if he sacrifices it to your opinion.' These are the words of which political figure, in his 1774 Speech to the Electors of Bristol?

Three bonus questions on Parliament. In each case, give the decade during which the following legislation was passed.

a. The Septennial Act, which increased the maximum length of a parliament from three years to seven. It was passed after a Jacobite uprising.

b. The Parliament Act, which reduced the maximum length of a parliament to five years? It also removed the power of the House of Lords to veto legislation.

c. The Fixed-Term Parliaments Act, which introduced fixed-term elections for the first time to the Westminster Parliament?

21 What did the German sociologist Max Weber define in 1919 as 'that entity which upholds the claim to the monopoly of the legitimate use of physical force in the enforcement of its order'?

Three bonus questions on abbreviations

a. Which organisation, sometimes known by its initials, was founded in 1935 by two men known as 'Bill W.' and 'Dr Bob S.'?

b. Often known by the same initials, the Automobile Association was founded in which decade?

c. For what do the letters A.A.A. stand in an abbreviation used in medicine to refer to a swelling in the wall of a central artery in the human body?

22 'Magazine', 'zenith', 'ghoul', 'giraffe' and 'sofa' are among English words that derive ultimately from which Semitic language?

Three bonus questions on football

a. Which club won the FA Cup five times in the trophy's first seven seasons, but was disbanded fewer than ten years after it won the trophy for the last time?

b. The first Football League competition took place in 1888–1889, and was won by which club, who won both the League and the FA Cup that season without losing a match?

c. Three clubs took part in both the first season of the Football League and the first season of the Premier League 104 years later. Name two of them.

23 Serving in both the Austro-Prussian and later the Franco-Prussian wars, which field marshal became the second president of the Weimar Republic in April 1925?

Three bonus questions on members of the United Nations

a. In addition to Egypt, three other African countries were original members of the UN: Ethiopia and South Africa were two; which West African country was the third?

b. Which original member of the UN held joint membership with Egypt between 1958 and 1961, before resuming individual membership?

c. Formerly part of Malaysia, which country achieved independence and became a separate member of the UN in 1965?

24 Probably born in the city of Miletus and listed by Plato as one of the Seven Sages, which mathematician, philosopher and astronomer was, according to Aristotle, the founder of physical science?

Three bonus questions on hop varieties

a. Which large group of traditional hop varieties shares its name with the author of *Pincher Martin* and *Lord of the Flies*?

b. Which traditional variety has a name that rhymes with words meaning 'adroitly balance several activities' and 'move into a warm, cosy position'?

c. Dating to the 1970s, which hop variety shares its name with the deepest known point in the oceans?

25 'The people who weep before my pictures are having the same religious experience I had when I painted them. And if you, as you say, are moved only by their colour relationships then you miss the point!' Which Latvian-born artist described his work with these words?

Three bonus questions on artists born in the 1880s

a. *Early Sunday Morning* and *Second Story Sunlight* are works by which US artist, active mainly in New York?

b. *The Bride of the Wind* and the *Prometheus* and *Thermopylae* triptychs are among works of which Austrian-born artist, who became a British citizen in 1946?

c. *Coming out of School*, *The Football Match* and *Peel Park, Salford* are works by which English artist?

26 The flag of which major world power consists of three horizontal bands that are the same colours, reading downwards, as the central section of the Irish tricolour, the hoist band of the French flag, and the fly band of the Belgian flag?

Three bonus questions on medicine

a. From the Greek for 'brought forth by a healer', what adjective describes a disease produced by a doctor or healthcare professional, for example, a side effect or complication resulting from a treatment?

b. What word describes an infection of animals that may be communicated to humans, an example being bovine tuberculosis?

c. What Greek-derived word describes those infections known as HAIS, that is 'hospital acquired' or 'healthcare associated'?

27 The discovery of the Earth's first co-orbital asteroid was announced in 2011; Jupiter, by comparison, has several thousand such objects, also known by what name, that of the people of an ancient city?

Three bonus questions on geology. In each case, give the name of the following economically important minerals.

a. What is the common name for calcium sulphate dihydrate? It is a soft white crystalline mineral, in bulk known as alabaster, and is used in making plaster of Paris.

b. Including muscovite and phlogopite, which group of minerals can be split along cleavage planes into very thin sheets, and are used as a dielectric in capacitors and as furnace inspection windows?

c. What is the common name of the mineral iron sulphide, which has been used in the paper industry to produce sulphur dioxide?

28 Expressed in kiloelectron-volts, electromagnetic radiation at what energy is an indicator of annihilating electrons and positrons, as seen for example in the region near our galactic centre?

Three bonus questions on biblical sacrifices

a. According to the Book of Genesis, who makes the first blood sacrifice acceptable to God, yielding up 'the first born of his flock and of their fat portions'?

b. Also in Genesis, who built an altar to God on which he sacrificed 'burnt offerings' taken from every clean animal and every clean bird?

    c.   Again in Genesis, which animal was used to take the place of Isaac after an angel prevented Abraham from carrying out the sacrifice of his own son?

29 Awarded the Nobel Prize in 1913, the Dutch physicist Heike Kamerlingh Onnes discovered which phenomenon, relating to the loss of electrical resistance at extremely low temperatures?

Three bonus questions on thermometry

    a.   After a scientist born in 1564, what name is given to a thermometer that indicates the temperature based on the motion of a collection of weights of varying densities suspended in a transparent liquid?

    b.   What name is given to the upward force exerted by a fluid that opposes the weight of a body suspended in it?

    c.   To what temperature on the Celsius scale does 50 degrees Fahrenheit correspond?

30 Deemed 'a symbol of universal goodwill', which creation prompted the League of Nations in 1935 to present a special medal to Walt Disney?

Three bonus questions on the words of Franklin D. Roosevelt. In each case give the three words that complete the following quotations.

    a.   First, from a speech of 1933: 'The only thing we have to fear ...'

    b.   Second, from December 1940: 'We have the men, the skill, the wealth, and above all, the will ... We must be the great ...'

    c.   Finally: 'Yesterday, December 7th, 1941 – a date which will ...'

The Answers

1 Pig

    a.   The Empress of Blandings

    b.   Old Major

    c.   Babe

2 Corsica

    a.   (Hugh) Latimer / (Nicholas) Ridley (not Thomas Cranmer, who was burned the following year)

    b.   Augsburg

    c.   (Emperor) Charles V (who was also Charles I of Spain)

3 Spanish Civil War

    a.   Australia (D.B.C. Pierre, 2003; Thomas Keneally, 1982; Peter Carey, 1988)

    b.   Ireland (John Banville, 2005; Anne Enright, 2007; Iris Murdoch, 1978)

    c.   India (Kiran Desai, 2006; Arundhati Roy, 1997; Aravind Aviga, 2008)

4 Twenty-five (five squared, of course)

    a.   Jean-Paul Sartre

    b.   (Karl) Jaspers

    c.   (Søren) Kierkegaard

5 'B' (Aden and Baden)

    a.   Chattel and chatter

    b.   Hovel and hover

    c.   Angel and anger

⑥ Saudi Arabia (becomes unique answer at the third country)
- **a.** Australia
- **b.** *The Shock of the New* (later updated as *The New Shock of the New*)
- **c.** (Francisco de) Goya

⑦ *The Turn of the Screw* (Henry James)
- **a.** Michael Chabon
- **b.** *Wonder Boys*
- **c.** Alaska

⑧ Doggerland (but not Dogger Bank)
- **a.** Imminent
- **b.** Backing
- **c.** Good

⑨ (Amedeo) Avogadro (1776–1856)
- **a.** Autograft
- **b.** Malpighian layer (after Marcello Malpighi)
- **c.** Sebaceous (glands)

⑩ St Nicholas (of Bari / of Myra; the prototype of Santa Claus)
- **a.** (Daniel) O'Connell
- **b.** Kilmainham (Gaol)
- **c.** General Post Office / GPO Building

⑪ *Hamlet* (Marcellus)
- **a.** Eglantine
- **b.** Woodbine
- **c.** Violet

⑫ 24
- **a.** Tribology (Greek: *tribos*, 'rubbing')
- **b.** Trichology (Greek: *trichos*, 'hair')
- **c.** Tribune (Latin: *tribus*, 'tribe')

⓭ Magna Carta
- **a.** Motor car
- **b.** Martyrdom
- **c.** Democracy

⓮ Brazil (China and the USA are both larger than Brazil, but border Russia and Canada, so do not fit the criterion)
- **a.** Cynic
- **b.** Mycroft Holmes (brother of Sherlock, of course)
- **c.** Hermit crabs

⓯ Tea
- **a.** Algeria and regalia
- **b.** Amherst and hamster
- **c.** Assam and amass

⓰ -land (Finland, Poland, Switzerland, Ireland)
- **a.** Prim
- **b.** Pire
- **c.** Emir

⓱ Pink / fuchsia / violet (pink to fuchsia for a pH range of 8.2–12.0, colourless above 12.0)
- **a.** Strontium (imparting a deep red colour; the village of Strontian)
- **b.** Technetium (atomic number 43)
- **c.** Molybdenum

⓲ Cretaceous and Tertiary
- **a.** Syncline
- **b.** Synchromesh
- **c.** Synapse

⓳ Jodrell Bank
- **a.** Sirius / Dog Star
- **b.** Tau Ceti

    c.   100 (3.5-(-1.44)=> 5=2.5log(100))

20 (Edmund) Burke
- **a.** 1710s (1715)
- **b.** 1910s (1911; a Parliament Act of 1949 further reduced the power of the Lords)
- **c.** 2010s (2011)

21 The State (in *Politics as a Vocation*, 1919)
- **a.** Alcoholics Anonymous
- **b.** 1900s (1905)
- **c.** Abdominal Aortic Aneurysm

22 Arabic
- **a.** Wanderers (Football Club)
- **b.** Preston (North End)
- **c.** Aston villa, Blackburn (Rovers) and Everton

23 (Paul von) Hindenburg
- **a.** Liberia
- **b.** Syria
- **c.** Singapore

24 Thales
- **a.** Golding (often seen in the plural, or preceded by an area, e.g. East Kent)
- **b.** Fuggle ('juggle' and 'snuggle')
- **c.** Challenger (the Challenger Deep in the Mariana Trench)

25 Mark Rothko
- **a.** (Edward) Hopper (1882–1967)
- **b.** (Oskar) Kokoschka (1886–1980)
- **c.** L.S. Lowry (1887–1976)

26 Russia (white, blue, red, of course)
- **a.** Iatrogenic (Greek: *iatros*, 'healer')

    b.   Zoonosis / zoonose
    c.   Nosocomial (Greek: *nosokomos*, 'person who attends the sick')

27 Trojans / Trojan asteroids
    a.   Gypsum
    b.   Mica
    c.   (Iron) pyrite (also nicknamed 'fool's gold', 'brass', 'brazzle', 'brazil')

28 511 (keV)
    a.   Abel (Cain's prior offering was not acceptable; Genesis 4: 3–8)
    b.   Noah (Genesis 8: 20, after the Flood)
    c.   Ram (accept sheep, lamb, correcting it, but not ewe; Genesis 22: 1–13)

29 Superconductivity
    a.   Galilean (thermometer)
    b.   Buoyancy
    c.   10 degrees Celsius

30 Mickey Mouse
    a.   '… is fear itself'
    b.   '… arsenal of democracy'
    c.   '… live in infamy'

Match Fourteen

1 According to the historian Robert Service, the Soviet state budgets would have been 'massively insolvent' for many years during the Brezhnev era had it not been for revenues derived from domestic sales of which product?

Three bonus questions on a language family

a. From the Latin for 'southern' and the Greek for 'island', what term denotes the language family that had the widest geographic span in pre-Columbian times? Sometimes known as 'Malayo-Polynesian', it currently has more than 300 million speakers.

b. The national language of which large island is the westernmost outlier of the Austronesian family? It was probably settled by people from Borneo from around AD 300.

c. Annexed by Chile in 1888, which isolated island is the easternmost outlier of the Austronesian family?

2 Born in 1561, the Italian physician Santorio Santorio pioneered the study of what chemical process in living organisms? It involves alternately building up complex molecules and breaking them down.

Three bonus questions on a spice

a. Associated particularly with northern and eastern Europe, which biennial herb bears fragrant seeds often added to sauerkraut and rye bread? They are used as the main flavouring in spirits such as akvavit and kummel.

b. Caraway belongs to the Apiaceae family. This family is usually known by the name of which common herb, used in salads, stuffings and bouquet garni?

c. Caraway is traditionally noted for its carminative properties, meaning that it may relieve or prevent what condition, often associated with the consumption of pulses or cruciferous vegetables?

3 What noun links the common name of the marine fish *Naucrates ductor*, the juveniles of which swim alongside boats or larger fish such as sharks, and the common name of a toothed black whale with a bulbous overhanging snout?

Three bonus questions on world rulers. I will read a list of rulers who were on the throne or in power during the first year of a century of the Common Era. In each case, I simply want the century.

a. Chandragupta II of India, Yazdegerd I of Sassanid Persia, and Alaric I of the Visigoths?

b. Magnus Barefoot of Norway, Baldwin II, Count of Edessa, and the Byzantine Emperor Alexius I Comnenus?

c. Emperor Kangxi of the Qing dynasty, the Mughal Emperor Aurang-Zeb, and Charles XII of Sweden?

4 The English opera *King Arthur* was a collaboration between the poet John Dryden and which composer?

Three bonus questions on pairs of composers born in the same year. In each case, name both the composers from the works listed.

a. The composers of the opera *Lucia di Lammermoor* and the Symphony Number 8 in B Minor, the 'Unfinished', both born in 1797?

b. The composers of the operas *Falstaff* and *Rienzi*, both born in 1813?

c. The composers of the *Karelia Suite* and *The Sorcerer's Apprentice*, both born in 1865?

5 Which Dutch artist coined the term 'neo-plasticism' in 1917 to describe his own style of abstract work, which he created using only the primary colours and black, grey and white?

Three bonus questions on Dutch art

a. In the collection of the National Gallery, *The Avenue at Middelharnis* is a work by which Dutch artist, born in 1638?

b. Which city west of Amsterdam was the birthplace of Jacob van Ruisdael? The interior of its cathedral is the subject of a noted work by Pieter Saenredam.

c. His works including *The Milkmaid* and *The Astronomer*, which painter is especially associated with the city of Delft, his birthplace in 1632?

6 William Henry Harrison, John Tyler, Zachary Taylor and Millard Fillmore are US presidents who shared what party affiliation?

Three bonus questions on presidents of the Royal Society

a. President of the Royal society from 1915 to 1920, which physicist revolutionised the knowledge of atomic structure by his discovery of the electron?

b. Which early twentieth-century president of the Royal Society gives his name to the dispersion of electromagnetic radiation by particles that have a radius less than approximately one-tenth the wavelength of the radiation?

c. Which pioneer of antiseptic surgery was president of the Royal Society from 1890 to 1895?

7 The single-word English name of which European country begins with four letters meaning 'symbol of authority of the House of Commons'?

Three bonus questions on British history. In each case, name the twentieth-century prime minister who was served by the following chancellors of the Exchequer.

a. Anthony Barber?

b. Philip Snowden?

c. Finally, David Lloyd George?

8 According to the title of his novelty song, Spike Milligan was 'walking backwards for Christmas, across ...' which stretch of water?

Three bonus questions on trading blocs

a. In December 2011, which South American trading bloc agreed to close its ports to ships flying the Falkland Islands flag?

b. What name was given to the agreement reached by Canada, Mexico and the USA in 1993 that made the three countries a free-trade area?

c. Established in 1834, the Zollverein Customs Union created a free-trade area throughout much of which modern-day country?

9. Which animal is being classified? Phylum: chordata; class: mammalia; order: rodentia; family: caviidae; genus: *cavia*; species: *Cavia porcellus*.

Three bonus questions on London museums

a. A house on Brook Street became the first London museum to be dedicated to a composer when it opened in 2001. To which German-born composer is it dedicated?

b. Located on Euston Road, which collection for 'the incurably curious' is named after the co-founder of a multinational pharmaceutical company?

c. Britain's National Museum of Aviation, the Royal Air Force Museum is set on over ten acres of land formerly belonging to which aerodrome?

10. Listen carefully. Using the substitution cipher where letters are replaced by their position in the alphabet, what four-letter word is represented by the string twenty-five, twenty-one, twelve, five?

Three bonus questions on the US architect Daniel H. Burnham

a. Completed by Burnham in 1902, which office building filled the triangular plot at the intersection of Fifth Avenue and Broadway? It has been called New York's oldest skyscraper.

b. For which US city did Burnham design the Reliance Building in 1895, and produce a 'master plan' in 1909, now considered a landmark in the history of urban planning?

c. Burnham co-designed which London department store, which opened on Oxford Street in 1909?

11 Published between 430 and 424 BC, the works of which historian were divided by later editors into nine books named after the Muses?

Three bonus questions on an EU member state

a. The Gulf of Finland separates Finland from the Russian Federation and which former Soviet republic?

b. A little smaller than the Western Isles, what is the largest island of Estonia and the second-largest in the Baltic Sea?

c. Estonia joined the Eurozone on 1 January of which year?

12 Adversely affecting fishing, agriculture and weather from Ecuador to Chile, what Spanish name denotes the anomalous appearance every few years of unusually warm ocean conditions along the west coast of South America?

Three bonus questions on the Minor Prophets of the Old Testament

a. Which prophet fled from the task of warning the inhabitants of Nineveh that it was to be destroyed by God? He then embarked on a sea voyage, during which he was swallowed by a great fish.

b. An execration of the Edomites for joining the enemies of Judah in sacking Jerusalem, what is the shortest book in the Old Testament?

c. After Haggai and Zechariah, what, in the Christian ordering, is the last book of the Old Testament?

13 What is the fourth largest island of the Greater Antilles, after Cuba, Hispaniola and Jamaica?

Three bonus questions on geography

a. After China, what is the most populous Asian country to have a larger population than any of its neighbours?

b. After Nigeria, what is the most populous African country to have a larger population than any of its neighbours?

c. Which is the only South American country whose population is larger than that of any country it borders?

14 Which artist was born in the Virgin Islands in 1830? He developed a friendship with Monet in 1859, and the two took refuge in Britain during the Franco-Prussian War. In 1872, he settled in Pontoise where he taught landscape painting to Cézanne, and he later became the only artist to participate in all eight Impressionist exhibitions.

Three bonus questions on a shared name

a. Newmanites and Puseyites were names given to members of which nineteenth-century movement, which sought a renewal of Catholic thought in the Anglican church?

b. Who, in 1258, led the barons' rebellion which forced Henry III to accept the Provisions of Oxford, establishing a new form of government in England?

c. Which monarch convened the Oxford Parliament, the third of the three parliaments of the Exclusion Crisis?

15 Binomially speaking, *Perdix perdix* in *Pyrus communis* form what seasonal pairing?

Three bonus questions on a plant family

a. The plant family Ericaceae includes which evergreen shrub, *Calluna vulgaris*, commonly found on moorlands in Britain?

b. What is the common name of *Vaccinium oxycoccus*, a plant of the Ericaceae family with red berries that are cultivated for their juice and for use in sauces?

c. Ericaceous compost is often made from what substance, formed by the partial decomposition of organic matter and traditionally used as fuel?

16 Between Turkey and Egypt, three independent sovereign nations have coastlines on the Mediterranean. For five points, name all three.

Three bonus questions on the Peloponnese

a. Give either the name of the ancient city state in the Peloponnese or the adjective deriving from it which means 'characterised by austerity or lack of comfort'?

b. Give either the name of the region of the Peloponnese or the adjective deriving from it which means 'sententiously brief', supposedly a characteristic of the people of the region?

c. Again, give either the name of the city in the Peloponnese or the adjective deriving from it which means 'excessively elaborate', and links an order of classical architecture and a number of originally amateur sports teams?

17 'Will you buy any tape?', 'Jog on, jog on, the footpath way' and 'When daffodils begin to peer' are all songs found in which of Shakespeare's plays?

Three bonus questions on vulgarity

a. 'To be more interested in the writer than the writing is just eternal human vulgarity.' These are the words of which British novelist, whose works include *Yellow Dog* and *Time's Arrow*?

b. 'Economy was always "elegant", and money-spending always "vulgar and ostentatious"; a sort of sour-grapeism, which made us very peaceful and satisfied.' These words appear in which novel of 1853 by Elizabeth Gaskell?

c. 'She is hard upon vulgarity; not, however, on good-natured vulgarity, such as that of Mrs Jennings ... but on vulgarity like that of Miss Steele.' These words refer to which novelist, born in 1775?

18 'There is nothing wrong with America that cannot be cured by what is right with America.' These are the words of which president, in his first inaugural address in January 1993?

Three bonus questions on writings on justice

a. Arguing for a principled reconciliation of liberty and equality, *A Theory of Justice* is a 1971 work by which US philosopher?

b. Which US philosopher gave a libertarian view of justice in the 1974 work *Anarchy, State and Utopia*, arguing for a minimal state and rejecting Rawls's idea of redistributive taxation?

c. 'Injustice anywhere is a threat to justice everywhere.' These are the words of which US political activist, in a letter of 1963?

19 Launched in 1975 and named after a group of seafarers, which NASA project was the first planetary exploration mission to transmit pictures from the surface of Mars?

Three bonus questions on tests for chemicals

a. What chemical species does the brown ring test detect?

b. Born in 1812, which German chemist's name is given to the two solutions, usually known as 'a' and 'b' which, when used together, are a test for reducing sugars or aldehydes?

c. What chemical species does the Marsh test detect?

20 What word is both an alternative name for a refractory metallic element, and the surname of the British scientist who designed the technical software suite Mathematica?

Three bonus questions on alloys

a. Phosphor bronze, an alloy used when resistance to wear and corrosion is important, is made from copper, phosphorus and which other element?

b. What is the principal metal in the alloy called gunmetal, which also contains zinc and tin?

c. Muntz metal consists of 60 per cent copper and 40 per cent zinc in the form of what alloy?

21 The isoperimetric problem of determining the greatest area enclosed by a closed plane curve of fixed perimeter is often named after which legendary figure, the first Queen of Carthage?

Three bonus questions on a poet

a. 'With Mozart and perhaps Goethe he can claim to be the greatest and most universal genius since the Renaissance.' These words of Isaiah Berlin refer to which Russian poet, born in 1799?

b. Based on the great flood of St Petersburg in 1824, which of Pushkin's poems relates the fate of the poor clerk, Evgeny, who imagines he is chased through the streets by the statue of Peter the Great?

c. Which of Pushkin's novels in verse inspired an opera by Tchaikovsky, a ballet by John Cranko, and Vikram Seth's verse novel *The Golden Gate*?

22 In physics, the process of converting alternating electrical current to direct current is known as what?

Three bonus questions on African capitals

a. Cotonou is the seat of government and Porto-Novo the official capital of which West African country? It gained independence from France in 1960.

b. Pretoria is the executive capital of South Africa and Cape Town the legislative; which inland city is the judicial capital?

c. Dodoma has been the designated capital of Tanzania since the 1970s, although the seat of much government administration has remained in which seaport?

23 In 2012, Lord Dyson succeeded Lord Neuberger as the holder of what senior judicial office?

Three bonus questions on the binomial theorem

a. In the polynomial expansion of the expression x-plus-one all raised to the power five ($(x+1)^5$), what is the coefficient of x^3?

b. What is the sum of the binomial coefficients 'n choose k', as k ranges from zero up to n, a quantity equal to the total number of subsets of an n-element set?

c. From the numbers 1 up to 1,000, how many sets consisting of 999 numbers can be formed?

24 Writing in defence of the Glorious Revolution, which English philosopher outlined his political theory by attacking the notion of the divine right of kings in the 1690 work *Two Treatises on Government*?

Three bonus questions on shorter words that can be made using any of the ten letters of the word 'absolutely'. In each case, give the word from the definition.

a. A large pill, or a small rounded mass of chewed food?

b. An administrative division of the Russian Republic, for example Samara, Rostov or Tomsk?

c. A three-letter word denoting a highly alkaline solution used for washing or cleansing?

25 Which work of 2010 by the US psychologists Christopher Chabris and Daniel Simons describes an experiment in 'inattentional blindness', in which volunteers were required to concentrate so intently on a video of basketball passes that almost half of them failed to see a woman dressed as a large ape walking among the players?

Three bonus questions on mammalian physiology

a. Known chemically as N-acetyl 5-Methoxytryptamine, which hormone has a role in establishing circadian rhythms?

b. Which endocrine gland secretes melatonin?

c. In the diurnal cycle, when are blood concentrations of melatonin at their highest?

26 In physical chemistry, Graham's law of diffusion states that the rate of diffusion of a gas at constant temperature and pressure is proportional to what?

Three bonus questions on chemistry

a. The winner of the Nobel Prize for Chemistry in 1903, which Swedish scientist defined an acid as a substance that can yield hydrogen ions when it dissociates in a solution?

b. Based on independently postulated theories by the Danish and English chemists after whom it is named, which definition of an acid describes it as a substance that can transfer a proton to another substance, such as the solvent when it occurs in solution?

c. In 1923, which US chemist gave an even more general definition of an acid as a substance with an affinity for electron pairs contributed by bases, which themselves contain unshared electron pairs?

27 'Novels of character and environment', 'Romances and fantasies' and 'Novels of ingenuity' are groups used by which literary figure to classify his prose works? After a novel of 1895 was harshly criticised, he turned to the writing of poetry.

Three bonus questions on authors and their pleasures

a. 'I am entitled to my share of light-heartedness, and there is nothing wrong with enjoying one's self simply, like a boy.' This remark of Leo Tolstoy refers to his learning to do what, at the age of 67?

b. 'Taming the Bicycle' is the title of an essay by which US humorist and author? It describes his attempts to master the vehicle during the early 1880s around his home town of Hartford, Connecticut.

c. Hoopdriver, a draper's assistant, and Jessie, a 'young lady in grey', share cycling idylls in *The Wheels of Chance*, a 1896 work by which prolific novelist?

28 Born in 1931, with which Soviet leader are the terms *glasnost*, meaning 'openness', and *perestroika*, meaning 'restructuring', most associated?

Three bonus questions on physics

a. The 1933 Nobel Prize in Physics was shared between two men, each of whom gives his name to an equation formulated within the previous ten years. Erwin Schrödinger was one; who was the other?

b. Dirac's Nobel Prize lecture concluded with these words: 'The two kinds of stars would show exactly the same spectra, and there would be no way of distinguishing them by present astronomical methods.' What was the difference between the two kinds of star he was discussing?

c. In Schrödinger's Nobel lecture, to what physical phenomenon was he referring when he said, 'We can easily hear a man calling from behind a high wall or around the corner of a solid house'?

29 Expressed in a book with the translated English title *Classic of the Way*, which philosophy, stressing the unity of humanity and the universe, was founded more than 2,000 years ago by Lao-Tzu?

Three bonus questions on rulebooks

a. First published in 1844, the book commonly referred to as 'Erskine May' is a reference work detailing the laws, privileges and procedures of which body?

b. Also known by the name of the peer who endorsed them, 'No shoes or boots with springs allowed' and 'No hugging' are among the rules drawn up in 1867 for which sport?

c. 'Of Obedience', 'Of Humility' and 'Of Excommunication for Faults' are chapters in the monastic rule of which saint, who gives his name to a major monastic order?

30 Victor Hugo, Charles Fourier and Pierre-Joseph Proudhon were all born in which French city, capital of the Doubs département, around 75 kilometres east of Dijon?

Three bonus questions on asexual reproduction in plants. I will describe three vegetative structures, and I want the botanical term for each.

a. The horizontal underground stem seen in stinging nettles; it grows and branches in soil, rooting at nodes to produce new plantlets.

b. The bud-like masses of cells, often in the form of cups or discs, that become detached and grow into new plants; they are characteristic of certain liverworts and some flowering plants, for example sundew.

c. Horizontal stems arising from axillary buds seen in plants such as strawberries; they grow along the surface of the ground and new plantlets arise from nodes.

The Answers

1 Vodka
- **a.** Austronesian (Latin: *australis*; Greek: *nesos*)
- **b.** Madagascar
- **c.** Easter Island / Rapa Nui

2 Metabolism (also known as Sanctorius of Padua)
- **a.** Caraway (*Carum carvi*; also called meridian fennel or Persian cumin)
- **b.** Parsley (*Petroselinum hortense*)
- **c.** Flatulence, wind (accept less formal alternatives, correcting gently)

3 Pilot (pilot fish and pilot whale)
- **a.** Fifth century / 401
- **b.** Twelfth century / 1101
- **c.** Eighteenth century / 1701

4 (Henry) Purcell
- **a.** Donizetti and Schubert
- **b.** Verdi and Wagner
- **c.** Sibelius and Dukas

5 (Piet) Mondrian
- **a.** (Meindert) Hobbema
- **b.** Haarlem
- **c.** (Jan) Vermeer

6 Whig

  a. (J.J.) Thomson (Joseph John Thomson, 1856–1940)
  b. (Lord) Rayleigh (John William Strutt, 3rd Baron Rayleigh;
     Rayleigh scattering)
  c. (Joseph) Lister

7 Macedonia ('mace', of course)
  a. (Edward) Heath (1970–1974)
  b. (James) Ramsay Macdonald (1924 and 1929–1931)
  c. (H.H.) Asquith (1908–1915)

8 The Irish Sea
  a. Mercosur / Merçado Común del Sur (Argentina, Brazil,
     Paraguay and Uruguay)
  b. NAFTA / North American Free Trade Agreement
  c. Germany

9 (Domestic) guinea pig / cavy
  a. (George Frideric) Handel (who had lived in it from 1723
     until his death in 1759)
  b. Wellcome Collection (after philanthropist Sir Henry
     Wellcome, 1853–1936)
  c. Hendon

10 Yule (25 = y, 21 = u, 12 = l, 5 = e)
  a. Flatiron Building / Fuller Building
  b. Chicago
  c. Selfridges

11 Herodotus
  a. Estonia
  b. Saaremaa
  c. 2011

12 El Niño (or El Niño-Southern Oscillation; 'the boy', of course,
   meaning the Christ child)
  a. Jonah

    b.   Obadiah
    c.   Malachi

13 Puerto Rico
    a.   Indonesia (India borders China, of course)
    b.   Ethiopia (the others are Egypt, Democratic Republic of Congo, Algeria and Ghana)
    c.   Brazil

14 Camille Pissarro (not Lucien Pissarro, his son)
    a.   Oxford (Movement)
    b.   (Simon) de Montfort (6th Earl of Leicester)
    c.   Charles II (the Exclusion Crisis of 1678–1681)

15 A partridge in a pear tree
    a.   Heather / ling
    b.   Cranberry
    c.   Peat

16 Israel, Lebanon, Syria
    a.   Sparta / spartan
    b.   Laconia / laconic
    c.   Corinth / Corinthian

17 *The Winter's Tale* (sung by Autolycus)
    a.   Martin Amis
    b.   *Cranford*
    c.   Jane Austen (characters in *Sense and Sensibility*; critic and historian Goldwin Smith)

18 Bill Clinton
    a.   John Rawls
    b.   (Robert) Nozick
    c.   Martin Luther King

19 Viking (1 and 2; the Explorer programme began in 1958 but none has visited other planets)
  a. Nitrate / nitrate ion (the presence of nitrate ion in solution)
  b. (Hermann von) Fehling (1812–1885)
  c. Arsenic (allow arsenic compound(s))

20 Wolfram (wolfram=tungsten; Stephen Wolfram)
  a. Tin
  b. Copper
  c. Brass

21 Dido (Dido's problem; in some versions she is called Elissa or Alyssa)
  a. (Aleksandr) Pushkin
  b. 'The Bronze Horseman'
  c. *Eugene Onegin*

22 Rectification
  a. Benin
  b. Bloemfontein
  c. Dar es Salaam

23 Master of the Rolls
  a. 10 (accept 5 choose 3 or 5 c 3)
  b. Two-to-the-power-n (2^n)
  c. 1,000

24 John Locke
  a. Bolus
  b. Oblast
  c. Lye

25 *The Invisible Gorilla (and Other Ways Our Intuition Deceives Us)*
  a. Melatonin

    b.   Pineal (gland or body; accept epiphysis cerebri, epiphysis or coronarium)

    c.   Night / hours of darkness / early hours of morning (allow midnight, correcting it; strictly around 2 a.m. to 4 a.m.)

26 The square-root of its density

    a.   (Svante) Arrhenius

    b.   Brönsted-Lowry (acid; Johannes Nicolaus Brönsted, 1879–1947; Martin Lowry, 1874–1936)

    c.   (Gilbert) Lewis

27 (Thomas) Hardy (the novel being *Jude the Obscure*, of course)

    a.   Ride a bicycle

    b.   Mark Twain

    c.   H.G. Wells (Herbert George Wells)

28 (Mikhail) Gorbachev

    a.   (Paul) Dirac (NB not Heisenberg, who won in 1932, or Pauli, who won in 1945)

    b.   One made of matter, the other antimatter

    c.   Diffraction

29 Taoism / Daoism

    a.   Parliament (accept but qualify House of Commons; *A Practical Treatise on the Law, Privileges, Proceedings and Usage of Parliament* by Thomas Erskine May)

    b.   Boxing (Marquess of Queensberry Rules)

    c.   St Benedict (Order of St Benedict / the Benedictines)

30 Besançon

    a.   Rhizome (allow rootstock)

    b.   Gemmae / gemma

    c.   Runners / stolon

Match Fifteen

1. After a general in the Mexican army during the Mexican-American War of 1846–1848, what name is given to the neighbourhood of San Francisco noted since the late 1960s as a centre of gay activism, and later for the career of the politician Harvey Milk?

Three bonus questions on a sixteenth-century pope

  a. Which pope gives his name to a reform of the Julian calendar introduced in 1582? It was finally adopted in Britain in 1752.

  b. Which event in Paris in August 1572 did Gregory celebrate with a Te Deum mass and the striking of a commemorative medal bearing the Latin words *Ugunottorum strages*?

  c. Built by Gregory in 1574, which palace in Rome has, since 1948, been the residence of the Italian president?

2. What designation links Leamington Spa in 1838, Tunbridge Wells in 1909 and Wootton Bassett in 2011?

Three bonus questions on the states of India

  a. In which populous state is the city of Varanasi, one of the seven sacred cities of Hinduism?

  b. Bordering Uttar Pradesh to the east, in which state is the city of Gaya, near which Shakyamuni Buddha attained enlightenment?

   c. The golden temple of Amritsar, the most important place of Sikh pilgrimage, is in which state?

3 Work this out before you buzz. If x equals pi radians, what is the value of sin x plus cos x plus tan x?

Three bonus questions on geometry. In each case, I want the name of the distance-preserving transformation of the plane described.

   a. An orientation-preserving transformation whose only fixed point is the origin, described via complex arithmetic as multiplication by e-to-the-power-i-theta, for some real theta.

   b. An affine-transformation which moves every point of the plane a constant distance in the same direction, described via complex arithmetic as addition of some complex number z.

   c. A transformation of the plane whose set of fixed points coincides with a line through the origin, the matrix of this transformation always having determinant minus one.

4 Quote: 'Even such is time, which takes in trust / Our youth, our joys, and all we have, / And pays us but with age and dust.' These are the first lines of the epitaph of which courtier and explorer, written by him the night before his execution in 1618?

Three bonus questions on pairs of present participles whose spelling differs by the substitution of a single letter for a double letter, for example 'stripping' and 'striping'. In each case, give both words from the definitions.

a. 'Grasping tightly' and 'complaining persistently'?

b. 'Hermetically sealing for preservation' and 'belabouring with bamboo or rattan'?

c. 'Wiping with absorbent material' and 'feeling apathetic or dejected'?

5 'I cannot forecast to you [its] action ... It is a riddle, wrapped in a mystery, inside an enigma.' Of which country did Winston Churchill say these words in October 1939?

Three bonus questions on the Orwell Prize for political writing

a. The winner of the Orwell Prize in 2007, *Having It So Good* by the historian Peter Hennessey is an account of Britain during which decade?

b. The 2010 winner, *Keeper: A Book about Memory, Identity, Isolation, Wordsworth and Cake*, is Andrea Gillies' journal of caring for a relative suffering from what disease?

c. Toby Harnden's 2012 Orwell Prize-winning work *Dead Men Risen* is subtitled *The Welsh Guards and the Defining Story of Britain's War in ...*' which country?

6 The Victoria Cross was introduced as the highest award for gallantry during which decade?

Three bonus questions on megafauna of the Pleistocene epoch

a. Members of which extinct genus of predators of the Pleistocene epoch are known collectively by the term 'sabre-toothed cat'?

b. Around the size of a modern elephant, the giant ground sloth is known by what name, from the Greek for 'great beast'?

c. Around the size of a rhinoceros, the extinct Diprotodon is the largest known member of which infraclass of mammals of the southern hemisphere?

7 A Nylander solution, containing bismuth sub-nitrate and Rochelle salt, is used to detect the presence of what specific substance in urine? The solution turns black in a positive reaction.

Three bonus questions on a German company

a. With a logo formed from its name in the form of a cross, which company introduced the first sulfa drug, Prontosil, in 1935, and developed polyurethane two years later?

b. Which mild non-narcotic analgesic was introduced by Bayer in 1899? Its use can reduce the risk of heart attack in high-risk individuals.

c. In 1898, Bayer became the first company to introduce as a commercial product which drug, a narcotic analgesic for use in pain and cough medications?

8 In November 2011, a NASA mission was launched to land and operate the car-sized rover *Curiosity* on the surface of which planet, to investigate whether it ever offered conditions favourable for microbial life?

Three bonus questions on the Olympic Games of 1904

  a. Its then relatively inaccessible location thought to have been responsible for the low proportion of foreign competitors, which city on the Mississippi hosted the Olympic Games in 1904?

  b. For what principal reason, relating to the design of the running track, was the 1904 Olympic 200-metre winner Archie Hahn able to set the relatively quick winning time of 21.6 seconds?

  c. For what unusual reason was Fred Lorz, the first man to cross the winning line, disqualified from the 1904 Olympic marathon?

9 The four-letter surname of which US novelist begins the names of a Latvian-born exponent of colour-field painting, a German financier born in 1743, and a large town between Sheffield and Doncaster?

Three bonus questions on dressmaking terms

  a. Also used in the roasting of meat, what term can denote large, temporary stitching used to join a seam?

  b. What term for a wedge-shaped piece of cloth is also used for a similarly shaped piece of land, and occurs occasionally in place names?

  c. What term, meaning a cut or line diagonal to the grain of a woven fabric, also means 'a slant or prejudice'?

10 'Shadows, ghosts, ruins and doppelgangers. A madwoman emerging from a Hampstead fog. The villain, Count Fosco, who keeps white mice in his pocket. Marian Halcombe, an intrepid heroine with, of all things, a light moustache ...' These words of the author Nicci French describe which novel of 1860?

Three bonus questions on a London churchyard

a. Buried in St Pancras Old Church churchyard, what is the surname of the composer with the forenames Johann Christian, known as the 'London' member of his family? He died in 1782.

b. The family tomb of which neo-classical architect in St Pancras Old Church churchyard is thought to have been an influence on Giles Gilbert Scott's design for the red telephone box? Born in 1753, he gives his name to a museum in Lincoln's Inn Fields.

c. Buried in the same churchyard, the sculptor John Flaxman was, from 1775, a noted designer of jasperware for which English potter?

11 The psychologist Philip Zimbardo is best known for a simulated prison experiment carried out in 1971 in which US university?

Three bonus questions on a nineteenth-century writer and diplomat

a. Sir John Bowring was the literary executor of which utilitarian philosopher, whose radical journal, the *Westminster Review*, he edited from 1824?

b. In 1854, Bowring became the fourth governor of which British colony? His policies contributed to the outbreak of the conflict sometimes known as the Second Opium War.

c. Bowring gives his name to a treaty of 1855, negotiated with King Rama IV, that opened which country to western influence and trade?

12 From a Latin word meaning 'fixed' or 'binding', what term denotes the process by which a legislative body approves a measure introduced by another body? An example is the need for the US Senate to give formal consent to treaties or agreements entered into by the executive.

Three bonus questions on economics

a. What two-word term refers to a lack of incentive to guard against risk when one is protected from its consequences, for example, by insurance, or when the potential burden will be borne by others?

b. *The Economics of Moral Hazard* is a work by which US Nobel laureate, also known for the 1971 work *Essays in the Theory of Risk-Bearing*?

c. In 2009, which Bank of England governor described government bailouts of the banking system as 'possibly the biggest moral hazard in history'?

13 'Idealized rational acceptability under epistemically ideal conditions' is a definition given by the US philosopher Hilary Putnam for what common five-letter word?

Three bonus questions on philosophers

a. While in prison awaiting execution for treason in around AD 524, the Roman statesman Boethius wrote which work, an imagined conversation between himself and an allegorical figure?

b. Which Dominican friar and astronomer was burnt at the stake for heresy in 1600? His works on cosmology argued that the Sun was merely one of an infinite number of stars in an infinite universe.

c. Known as the 'Angelic Doctor', which Dominican priest and scholastic philosopher left his work the *Summa Theologica* unfinished on his death in 1274?

14 *Toward an Architecture* and *When the Cathedrals Were White* are among the works of which architect, born in Switzerland in 1887?

Three bonus questions on motorways

a. The A1 motorway in Croatia connects Zagreb to which Adriatic port, the country's second largest city, before continuing towards Dubrovnik?

b. The Austrian A1 motorway links Vienna with which city, lying over 250 kilometres to the west, close to the German border?

c. Also known as the Autoroute du Nord, the A1 in France connects Paris with which city 211 kilometres away?

15 31 July 1970 became known as Black Tot Day following the abolition of what tradition in the Royal Navy?

Three bonus questions on tranquillity

a. 'Poetry is the spontaneous overflow of powerful feelings: it takes its origin from emotion recollected in tranquillity.' These lines by Wordsworth appear in the preface to the 1802 edition of which anthology?

b. In the 1868 work 'Lucretius', which poet wrote: 'Passionless bride, divine tranquillity, / Yearned after by the wisest of the wise'?

c. 'Fame and tranquillity can never be bedfellows.' Which French thinker made this observation in his *Essais*, published from 1580?

16 Meanings of which five-letter word include: an arc with angle less than 180 degrees; the determinant of a matrix obtained by deleting one or more rows and columns; and the smaller of two differently derived versions of the same musical interval?

Three bonus questions on unfinished operas

a. Which Austrian composer left the orchestration of the third act of his 12-tone opera *Lulu* incomplete when he died in 1935?

b. A virtuoso pianist, which Italian-born composer's magnum opus is *Doktor Faust*, an opera he left incomplete on his death in 1924?

c. Which one-word title is shared by a Busoni opera of 1917 and the opera that Puccini left unfinished on his death in 1924?

17 Listen carefully and answer as soon as your name is called. In an ideal gas consisting of molecules with mass m, if the mass of the molecules is increased by a factor of four, by what factor is the speed of sound in the gas changed?

Three bonus questions on scientific laws

a. Born in Ireland in 1627, which scientist gives his name to law which states that, at constant temperature, the volume of a given mass of gas is inversely proportional to pressure?

b. Two German-born physicists give their names to the law of photochemical equivalence which states that each quantum of radiation absorbed in a photochemical process causes a single reaction. One is Einstein; who is the other, a leader of the pro-Nazi Deutsche Physik movement?

c. Using modern terminology, whose first law proposes that during meiosis the two members of any pair of alleles possessed by an individual will separate to different gametes and subsequently into different offspring?

18 Christmas Day 1950 saw the removal by four Scottish students of what object from Westminster Abbey? It turned up in Scotland the following April.

Three bonus questions on an author

a. In 2011, which novelist won the Man Booker Prize having been shortlisted on three previous occasions?

b. In which novel by Barnes does Geoffrey Braithwaite seek a stuffed bird that once inspired a French novelist?

c. Barnes's 2005 historical novel *Arthur and George* features which author as the hero in a story based on real events?

19 The name of what popular form of theatre originates from that of performers in ancient Greece and Rome who represented mythological stories through gestures and actions, the name translating literally as 'imitates all'?

Three bonus questions on US presidents

a. Which president assumed office in 1837, and was the first US president not born a British subject, or of British ancestry?

b. Who was the first vice president to assume office after the death of the president? This followed the demise of William Harrison in 1841.

c. Who was the first president to have his inaugural ceremony broadcast live on the internet?

20 A form of nativity play, *Bariona, ou le Fils du tonnerre* was the work of which literary figure? Written and performed in 1940 while its author was a prisoner of war, it was followed by *The Flies* and *No Exit*.

Three bonus questions on American photographers

a. Married to the painter Roland Penrose, which photographer, born in 1907, is remembered both for her fashion shoots and for her evocative photographs of the liberation of Paris in 1944?

b. Together with her huddled children, Florence Owen Thompson, an impoverished pea-picker in California, became the subject in 1936 of *Migrant Mother*, the most celebrated image of which photographer?

c. Best known for her work for *Rolling Stone* and *Vanity Fair*, Annie Leibovitz took the last portraits of which performer on the day he died in December 1980?

21 Their exact locations undisclosed, and regarded as representing the primary virtues of valour, wisdom and benevolence, the Mirror, the Sword and the Jewel form the sacred regalia of the monarchy of which country? Its lineage is said to go back more than 2,500 years.

Three bonus questions on pairs of words whose spelling differs only by the addition of a final letter 'o', for example 'cell' and 'cello'. In each case, give both words from the definitions.

a. A four-letter prefix meaning 'church', common in Welsh place names, and a Spanish word for a treeless, grassy plain, for example, in West Texas?

b. A school of Buddhism that employs paradoxical statements known as *Koan*, and a Greek philosopher from Elea who formulated paradoxes to defend the theories of Parmenides?

c. The simple past form of a common auxiliary verb, and a queen of Carthage whose death is recounted in the fourth book of Virgil's *Aeneid*?

22 Thought to date to the thirteenth century, and described by J.B. Priestley in his *English Journey* in 1933, the fair held annually in Nottingham in the first week of October is named after what bird?

Three bonus questions on oddities of English spelling

a. The Gaelic-derived name of which member of the grouse family is spelt with an initial silent letter, originally added to suggest Greek etymology?

b. Which short word has a silent third letter inserted to link it to a Latin word with the same meaning? It is rendered as 'trespasses' in some versions of the Lord's Prayer.

c. What common geographical term has, since the fifteenth century, been spelt with a silent letter after the first vowel to make it resemble Latin and French words with the same meaning?

23 'The American public does not laugh. It buys!' Attributed to the art dealer Paul Durand-Ruel, these words refer to the enthusiasm in the USA for the work of which school of painting, following a breakthrough exhibition in New York in 1886?

Three bonus questions on the arts. In each case, give the decade that links the following

a. Constable's *The Hay Wain*, De Quincey's *Confessions of an English Opium Eater* and the first performance of Beethoven's Ninth Symphony?

b. Manet's *Dejeuner sur l'herbe*, Dostoevsky's *Crime and Punishment* and the first performance of Brahms's German Requiem?

c. Oscar Wilde's *The Ballad of Reading Gaol*, Edvard Munch's *The Scream* and the first performance of Dvorak's New World Symphony?

24 Which imperial unit is equivalent to 259 hectares?

Three bonus questions on prime ministers. In each case, name the twentieth-century prime minister whose Cabinet included the following as home secretary and foreign secretary, respectively.

a. Sir William Joynson-Hicks and Austen Chamberlain?

b. James Chuter Ede and Ernest Bevin?

c. William Whitelaw and Lord Carrington?

25 Fairyhouse, Naas and Leopardstown are among racecourses that lie close to which European city?

Three bonus questions on the city of Dublin

a. The two components of the name 'Dublin' have the same meaning as those of the name of which English town, located around 135 miles away across the Irish Sea?

b. After an annual fair that was outlawed in the 1850s, the name of which area of Dublin has come to mean a scene of uproar or disorder?

c. *The Shadow of a Gunman* is the first in the so-called Dublin Trilogy of plays by which Irish writer, born in 1880?

26 The last four letters of the full name of which twin-island Caribbean country are the first four letters of a capital on the River Danube, around 200 kilometres south-east of Vienna?

Three bonus questions on the colour purple

a. A purple-and-green Sisserou parrot appears on the flag of which Caribbean island state?

b. A horizontal band of the heraldic colour murrey, or reddish-purple, appeared at the bottom of the flag of which republic, overthrown by force of arms in the late 1930s?

c. The flag of which international organisation has a purple background with a white fleur-de-lys inside a knotted rope?

27 Answer as soon as your name is called. You add together the number of books in the Harry Potter and Chronicles of Narnia series. What number results?

Three bonus questions on statues of fictional characters

a. Statues of which literary character were unveiled at Meiringen in Switzerland and the mountain resort of Karuizawa in Japan in 1988, some years before the unveiling of a statue near his fictional London home?

b. Funded by the author who created him, a statue of which fictional character appeared in Kensington Gardens in 1912?

c. Which character created by Michael Bond is commemorated in a statue unveiled at a major London railway station in 2000?

28 After a US anatomist born in 1928, what two-word term denotes the maximum number of times a population of normal human cells can divide?

Three bonus questions on cell biology

a. What mononuclear cells are responsible for bone formation?

b. What term denotes the large multinuclear cells responsible for bone resorption?

c. What term denotes amoeboid cells with histamine, serotonin and heparin granules that have an important role in allergy and anaphylaxis?

29 After a headland in Corsica where the Royal Navy first encountered such defences, what name was given to the circular forts erected around the English coast during the Napoleonic Wars?

Three bonus questions on transuranic elements. In each case, I want the scientist who gives his name to the following.

a. The element with atomic number 100 and chemical symbol Fm?

b. The element with atomic number 106 and chemical symbol Sg?

c. The element with atomic number 112 and chemical symbol Cn?

30 To the nearest billion years, according to analysis of data from the Wilkinson Microwave Anisotropy Probe satellite, and also the formula known as 'Hubble time', what is the best current estimate of the age of the universe?

Three bonus questions on science fiction

a. Which US author, who died in 2009, created the planet Riverworld, on which everyone who has ever lived comes back to life, leading to meetings such as the one between Mark Twain and Cyrano de Bergerac?

b. The egalitarian world of Anarres is the setting of which novel by Ursula K. Le Guin, subtitled *An Ambiguous Utopia*?

c. Purpose-built space habitats known as 'orbitals' are the home of billions of inhabitants in the 'Culture' novels of which Scottish author?

'It was my first experience of being on television and I was supremely nervous. You don't know whether you're going to get some awful rush of blood to the head and buzz too early and keep getting it wrong, or that you're going to be so inhibited you won't buzz at all even when you know the answer.'

STEPHEN FRY
(actor, writer)
Contestant, 1980

The Answers

1 (The) Castro (José Castro, 1808–1860)
- **a.** Gregory XIII (prompt for regnal number if 'Gregory')
- **b.** St Bartholomew's Day Massacre (the Latin meaning 'massacre of the Huguenots')
- **c.** Quirinal (Palace) / Quirinale

2 Royal
- **a.** Uttar Pradesh
- **b.** Bihar
- **c.** Punjab

3 Minus one
- **a.** Rotation
- **b.** Translation / shift
- **c.** Reflection

4 (Sir Walter) Raleigh
- **a.** Gripping and griping
- **b.** Canning and caning
- **c.** Mopping and moping

5 Russia / Soviet Union (in the quote he says Russia, though it was of course the USSR at the time)
- **a.** 1950s
- **b.** Alzheimer's (accept dementia, of which Alzheimer's in the most common form)
- **c.** Afghanistan

6 1850s (1856; after the Crimean War)
    a. Smilodon
    b. Megatherium
    c. Marsupials / Metatheria (not Monotremes: this is an order. Also known as the giant wombat)

7 Glucose ($C_6H_{12}O_6$; D-glucose, dextrose, grape sugar)
    a. Bayer (Prontosil being the first antimicrobial antibiotic drug)
    b. Aspirin / acetylsalicylic acid
    c. Heroin (not morphine or codeine)

8 Mars
    a. St Louis
    b. The race was run on a straight track / the track had no bends or corners (when run on part of an outdoor 400-metre track it begins on the curve)
    c. He received a lift in a car for part of the course

9 (Philip) Roth (Rothko, Rothschild and Rotherham, of course)
    a. Basting
    b. Gore
    c. Bias

10 *The Woman in White* (by Wilkie Collins; 'Nicci French' is a husband-and-wife writing team: Nicci Gerrard and Sean French)
    a. Bach
    b. (Sir) John Soane
    c. (Josiah) Wedgwood

11 Stanford (the Leland Stanford Junior University)
    a. (Jeremy) Bentham (1748–1832)
    b. Hong Kong
    c. Siam / Thailand

12 Ratification (Latin: *ratus*, fixed)

a. Moral hazard
b. (Kenneth J.) Arrow
c. Mervyn King

13 Truth

a. *Consolation of Philosophy* / *De Consolatione Philosophiae* (accept *The Consolations of Philosophy*, correcting it – that's Alain de Botton's 2000 work; Boethius converses with Lady Philosophy)
b. Giordano Bruno / Il Nolano
c. (St Thomas) Aquinas

14 Le Corbusier (1887–1965; Charles-Edouard Jeanneret)

a. Split
b. Salzburg
c. Lille

15 The Rum Ration

a. *Lyrical Ballads*
b. Alfred, Lord Tennyson
c. (Michel de) Montaigne (1533–1592)

16 Minor

a. Alban Berg
b. (Ferruccio) Busoni
c. *Turandot*

17 It is halved / 0.5 (the speed of sound is proportional to $1/\text{root}\{m\}$)

a. (Robert) Boyle
b. (Johannes) Stark (1874–1957; Stark-Einstein law, formulated independently, unsurprisingly)
c. (Gregor) Mendel (1822–1884)

18 The Stone of Scone (accept Stone of Destiny, Scottish Gaelic Lia Faíl; also known in England as the Coronation Stone)

a. Julian Barnes (for *The Sense of an Ending*)

b. *Flaubert's Parrot*
c. Arthur Conan Doyle

19 Pantomime (Greek: *pantominos*)
    a. Martin van Buren
    b. John Tyler
    c. Bill Clinton

20 (Jean-Paul) Sartre
    a. Lee Miller (Elisabeth Miller, Lee [Lady] Penrose)
    b. Dorothea Lange
    c. John Lennon

21 Japan
    a. Llan- and Llano
    b. Zen and Zeno
    c. Did and Dido

22 Goose / Nottingham Goose Fair
    a. Ptarmigan
    b. Debt(s)
    c. Island (Old English: 'igland'; Middle English: 'iland')

23 Impressionism
    a. 1820s (1821, 1821–1822, 1824)
    b. 1860s (1863, 1866, 1868)
    c. 1890s (1898, 1893, 1893)

24 Square mile (an acre is 0.405 hectares)
    a. (Stanley) Baldwin (all three from 1924 to 1929)
    b. (Clement) Attlee (all three from 1945 to 1951)
    c. (Margaret) Thatcher (1979–1983 and 1979–1982, when Carrington resigned)

25 Dublin
    a. Blackpool

    b.   Donnybrook

    c.   Sean O'Casey (the others being *Juno and the Paycock* and *The Plough and the Stars*)

26 Antigua and Barbuda (Budapest, of course)

    a.   Dominica

    b.   Spain

    c.   Scouting

27 Fourteen (seven of each)

    a.   Sherlock Holmes

    b.   Peter Pan

    c.   Paddington (Bear)

28 Hayflick limit (or Hayflick phenomenon; i.e. between 40 and 60 times; Dr Leonard Hayflick)

    a.   Osteoblasts

    b.   Osteoclasts / clast (cells; resorption being the process by which a structure is remodelled)

    c.   Mast cells / mastocytes

29 Martello Towers (Mortella Point)

    a.   (Enrico) Fermi (fermium)

    b.   (Glenn) Seaborg (seaborgium)

    c.   (Nicolaus) Copernicus (copernicium)

30 Fourteen (billion; the 'exact' figure is either 13.7 billion or 13.84 billion, give or take *c.*140 million years)

    a.   Philip José Farmer (five novels from 1971 to 1983)

    b.   *The Dispossessed*

    c.   Iain M. Banks

'I've heard universities say
that winning *University Challenge*
gave them more positive publicity
than when one of their faculty
won a Nobel Prize.'

SEAN BLANCHFLOWER
Contestant, 1995

'Before the recording we
went to have a drink in the
local pub. And when I say we
had a drink, that's probably an
understatement. We probably
had several drinks, and the effect
of this was that our nervous
disposition totally disappeared.
We couldn't care less what
happened, and in the context of
University Challenge that couldn't
have been better: we were
carefree and careless – and won
the match.'

MALCOLM RIFKIND
(former Foreign Secretary)
Contestant, 1967

'I had several drinks in the
pub beforehand, mainly barley
wine which was a real student
drink because it packed a huge
punch per penny. And the other
great thing was that you could
smoke, and I puffed my way
through a packet of twenty
No. 6, and my parents were
appalled watching this at home.
There was this revolting-looking
youth with terrible shaggy hair, I
looked like a female impersonator
wearing a very ill-fitting wig under
clouds of smoke, and half-cut
as well. I don't know how they
survived the shame of it.'

SEBASTIAN FAULKS
(novelist)
Contestant, 1972

'Some teams do take it seriously – too seriously, I would say – but the majority, the nicest teams, the *best* teams are the ones who obviously want to do well, but realise it's only a game.'

JEREMY PAXMAN
Presenter, 1994 to date